Sliding several kiln-g
of a complex orie
third-square meter lid.
poster; it read:

WANTED
DEAD or ALIVE
Alias: TEX BUDA
1876

Reward $40,000.00

Its faded, etched print showed a smiling old man, who wore a hand-hitched leather hat.

Below his name and the date of, 1876, was a hazardous warning: " ...*never, never look into his pale blue eyes!*"

Copyright 2010 by Jim Matheson
www.Texbuda.com
www.TexbudaBrand.com
www.TexbudaBrandClothing.com

All rights reserved. No part of this book may be reproduced by any information storage and retrieval system or transmitted in any form or by any means, electronic, mechanical, photocopying, recording or otherwise, except by a reviewer who may quote brief passages in a review, without written permission of the publisher.

Printed in the United States of America
First Printing: June 2010

ISBN 978-0-9679775-1-5

Book and Cover Design by Crystal Wood
Cover and "Wanted Poster" Photos of "Tex Buda" by Courts Griner
Photo of Annapurna in the Himalayas: BigStockPhoto.com

Tattersall Publishing
1155 Union Circle #308194
Denton, TX 76203
www.tattersallpub.com

ALIAS: TEX BUDA

by
Jim Matheson

Jim Matheson

TATTERSALL
PUBLISHING
Denton, Texas

To Buddy Morgan and his son, Dylan.

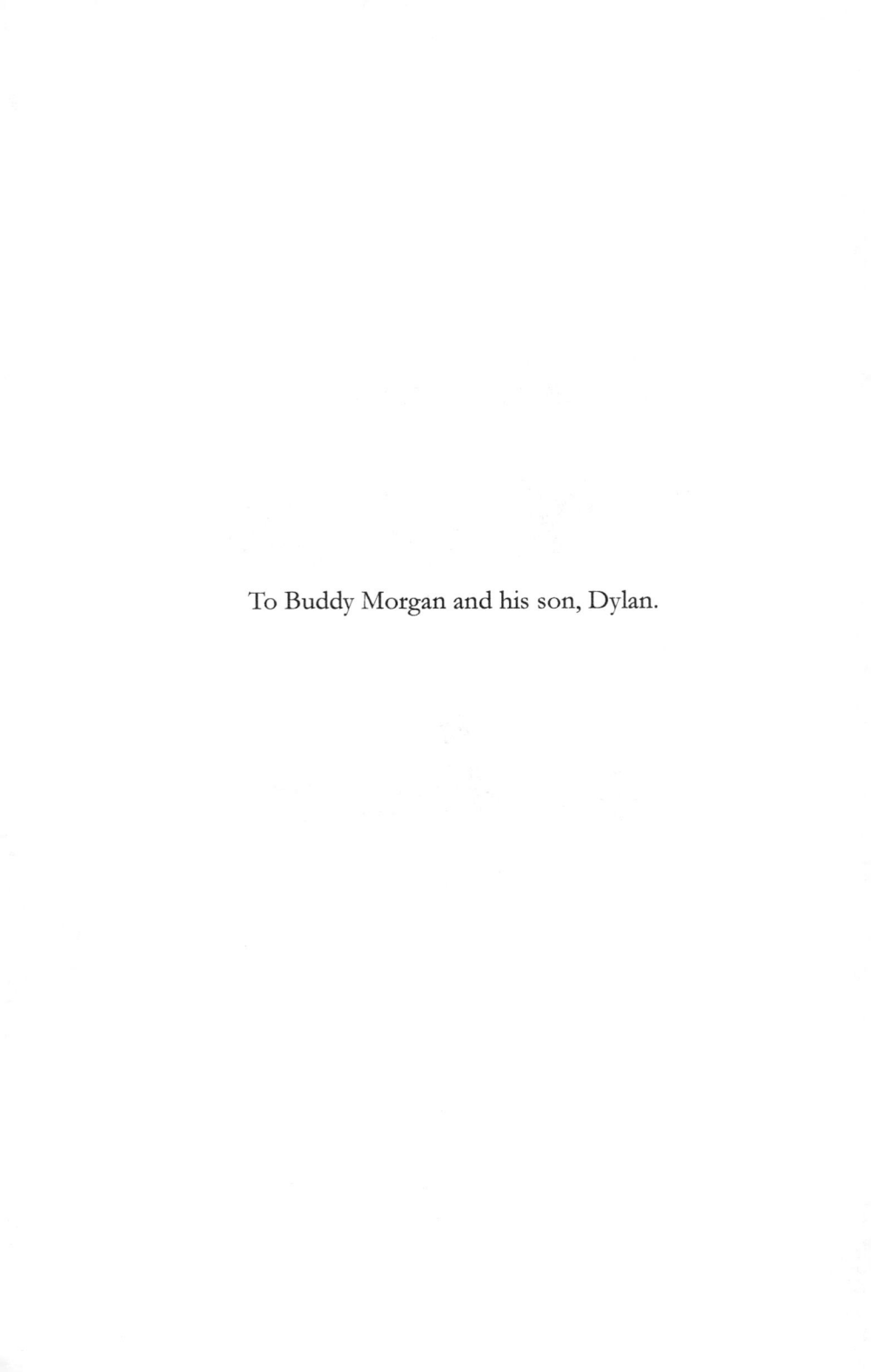

CHAPTER ONE

A few weeks ago of late Texas Winter, which was more like springtime, I traveled to a Benton, Arkansas mental institution, from a place called, Denton, Texas. Between Osama, Obama, and Chelsea's Mama, this presidential race was likely going to start another civil, or state-side war if anybody was hell-bent on assassination.

I had to meet my Grandma Lorena Rose Morgan for the first and last time. She was a fiercely independent, tough ole bird. I'd never have known her, 'cept a Jack Mormon genealogy bug bit me on the butt-end of a family history search in a Buda, Texas cemetery.

I'd asked a caretaker of the graves, "I'm looking for kinfolk's history. Do you have some graves marked *Morgan*?"

He told me, "Yep! There's two in the paupers section and one near the middle. Hop in my truck an' I'll show you."

At the paupers area, he showed me two old and faded plain white stones with the names *Sam* and *Tex*. Next, he showed me a third grave. It was nice, with a pretty rose quartz headstone bearing the name *Everest*.

I asked, "Do you by chance know who paid for all the stonework?"

While scratchin' his possum-head, he recalled, "Benton! Benton, Arkansas! That's where the bills were paid from... ...somethin', somethin' sharpening tools...you'll maybe find your kinfolk there, if they're still alive."

I thanked him with a twenty-buck tip and headed north.

In Benton, Arkansas, I found an ad in the Yellow Pages for Rose's Tools – 'Sharper than Thorns'. The sign in her front yard was overgrown with untended grass and weeds. Fortunately, a neighbor woman said, "Crazy witch, we had her put in the Institute's Rest Home."

Once there, it took a few slow breaths before I could get use to the inside air's sharpness of piddle and poop cleaners. I got directions by only asking a nurse named Aubrey, "Rose?"

The plaque on her shared room was decorated with a snow-capped mountain peak, within a climbing rose-carved frame.

After three knocks, I entered softly. One lady was curled up in a fetal ball and fast asleep under linen sheets. The other woman sat in a rocker near the silence of the room's only window.

She didn't turn until I asked, "Grandma Rose?"

She stopped rocking back and forth, turned her head to tip up her chin and stared at me with disbelief. "By the Gods, I always felt they'd missed killing all my men…always believed Tiex's Dragon Promise, 'You'll always be left with one more'."

Shaking her hand gently, I introduced myself, "I'm James Perry 'Buddy' Morgan." I shuffled over an empty chair while she reached for both my hands and felt the shape of my face, chin and nose. Last of all, she bent over on her knees and felt the size of my boots before sitting back up straight to kiss both my hands and begin to cry strange words, like a chant or prayer.

Within moments, I asked if I could record her stories.

She began smiling, giggled an infectious laughter and sang an answer of agreement, "As all the Gods and luck would have it so."

I began by telling her the names of three Morgan men who were in the Buda, Texas Cemetery. Grandma Rose seemed to clutch her chest and heave a big rock of questions from her heart. She covered her mouth and bit on her fist before composing herself again.

While recording our conversation, she thanked me for finding the Texas cemetery where she'd only known of her brother, Everest and "most of her husband" was buried.

With a few more tears, she added, "I had no idea my Daddy and Uncle Tex were killed there, too."

"Killed, Rose?"

"Sure enough to bet on a pile of chewed spit! He was a fist-beater, my husband; I only knew he'd killed my brother, but not Daddy and my uncle, too."

She paused a thoughtful minute of memory then confessed, "He forgot he had to fall asleep sometime. I duct-taped his hands to his crotch like a big diaper and shoved a lit stick of Hercules up his…well, you get the picture."

Stunned at her confession, but almost laughing, I had no idea her mother was still alive, being eighty years old herself.

She said her Mom was known only as Annie, for Annie Buda-Cole-Morgan. "But, I hain' seen or spoken to family 'ceptin' my brother, since runnin' away at fifteen."

She cried some more and I handed her my handkerchief. While blowing her nose, I expected neither lady'd have nothing to do with being put up in the nearest local old folks homes without a helluva fight.

"Jail-birds!" Granny Rose cackled with an effervescent humor, "They's who needs to live here...don't know how to care for 'emselves anyway...just wanta watch me die before passin' over the Rim of Heaven...just wanta fetch all the last drops of Medicare and Medicaid money they can drain from me afore then!"

Granny Rose gave me several reasons to continue my family history search. Pouring us each a glass of lemonade, she asked, "What's the difference between a, 'Hollow' and a 'Smoke Hole'?"

"OK, Grandma Rose—Moonshine?"

"Yeah, right...no, Buddy, a 'Hollow's back in the hills...a 'Smoke Hole' is *way* back."

"Grandma Rose, what are you trying to tell me?"

"You're searching for your history in a, hollow, Buddy; you need to search farther back in a Smoke Hole."

She continued after a shared chuckle of bewilderment, "Bryan, my only son, died after Korean combat, on a Matchless 500 motorcycle while scrambling up and down Fresno, California's dry irrigation canals. My grandson, Jimmy, the only grandson I knew of before you showed up today, died after Southeast Asia, in the rain forests of Central America. You being here means Jimmy met your mamma somewhere."

I replied, "What mamma told me about him wasn't very admirable. He was mean and knew all the martial arts, besides being a Sniper."

"Mamma was a world traveler. I loved it. I learned several languages. She made sure I understood the grammar of each, too. She lives in Houston, Texas now."

Rose rocked forward to lean on me. She hushed whispered words, "I wish I could've known her, too. If you was to be my heir, you'd need to know who you're come from. There's always good and bad in each of us, so don't let go of reins on the good. If the graves in Buda, Texas is supposed to be where my father and uncle are, too; they'd gone to seek out and deliver revenge on my husband and never came back…murdered, sure enough!"

Rose wagged her head back and forth in unsettled disbelief before going on, "I never knew the whys of it all. It had something to do with cleaning the riff-raff what burned down my mammas' home in Washington State. The graves there in Buda stretch back halfway 'round the world. I already told you most and some truth of who, what and where they were about. Trouble is, those questions and answers are only in 'The Hollows'."

"Grandma Rose, are you saying the answers to my history and these other mysteries, are in a Washington State 'Smoke Hole?'"

She answered loud again before finishing in her whisper, "Well, you might be the sharpest blade in a bucket of rusty knives, after all!" Then shushing, "You are exactly correct, except for your future's child. My penny-pinched fortune, home, farm, and Jimmy's set of his Daddy's two wheels are to be yours. But, your true treasure is the heritage, what me and Great-Grandma Annie will teach."

I checked my recorder and leaned close to her little rocking chair's arm. Rose told me, "There's a legendary 1800's character from Nepal, who under commission from the

King's prime minister, left his job as 1st Royal Bodyguard in Khatmandu to track some no-goods halfway around the world.

"His name was Tiex Buda. His mission was to protect the royal prince named Khrough, and deliver retribution for atrocities committed on his and the Kings' family members; Tiex Buda's parents had died as well. They were murdered way back in the 1800's. Nepal invaded India in 1813 and fought against four British East India Company Regiments until making a treaty in 1816."

Granny Rose called him a "Son of Dragons.' They were legendary mercenaries and royal bodyguards."

She fired me up. How could I stop my search? We sipped some more lemonade and I commented, "This lemonade have something else in it?"

Snickering, "Sure does. Aubrey, my little nurse angel, spikes it with vinegar and fruit jar junction's tea. Call Aubrey in here. I need a witness so my solicitor knows its you is my only grandson and heir."

I pressed the call buzzer and waited for the nurse's voice to answer.

"Rose, what do you need?"

Rose answered urgently, "Aubrey, I need you to witness for my new will. Please bring me a pen and paper."

Aubrey tapped on the door before walking in for introductions. When Rose finished dictating for Aubrey's transcription, we all signed the new documents, then Rose repeated the information into my recorder, with Aubrey and me giving statements of record.

"Do you need me to stay, Rose? I've got rounds to do."

Squeezing her hands, Rose answered, "You've been my best girl. Good-bye, Aubrey."

As she left us alone after checking on Rose's roommate, I took a slower sip of lemonade this time as Rose went on with her yarnin';

"…In 1876, they'd built a home near Little Annapurna in the Alpine Meadow Wilderness of the Washington State's Wenatchee Mountain Range. It wasn't made of the same rich materials; he reduced the size, but he built his place after the pattern of the four-story King's Palace in Khatmandu."

Granny Rose's eyes welled up, "On Friday the 13th of November 1909, the same year Indian Head pennies changed to Abe Lincolns, Mom was born there. After a couple generations of good neighbors passed away, narrow-minded kids persecuted 'em as witches and devils because they'd always been friends to Mormons.

"Mom was sick in a doctor's ward getting her tonsils taken out. On that night, a Trick or Treat mob showed up; they burned our little palace to the ground.

"Tales still speak of being run off by a Bigfoot and a Dragon. A local logging family named Cole adopted and raised Mamma after never finding a trace of her parents' bodies. She grew up an' got education at Bellingham's Teacher's College and taught English after I was born."

Of all else, Granny Rose told me, "There's a hidden treasure amongst the burned out ruins. It's supposed to be something called, 'dragons' eyes,' and maybe much more."

She went on to carefully describe, "...A hearth of stone with some kind of combination in the patterns of the furnace-fired ceramic glazed tiles, like flat, key-chain puzzles, but what's the combination? The palace-sized home was a crumbled pile after all the timbers burned out."

Granny Rose paused with her eyes closed, kind of dropped off to sleep, then opened wide-eyed at me, big blue eyes like pools of glacier water, "Tiex Buda was married to seven wives—not the Mormon's kinds of wives; Himalayan people also have plural wives ...one at a time, you understand...two or more in the same bed's sinnin'!"

Resting her eyes closed again and breathing slow and deep. I took her empty lemonade glass and set it on the window ledge. I thought she'd gone to sleep but she whispered, "Your Grandma Annie and me are named after Tiex's youngest and seventh wife, Lorena Annapurna...it was the first six wives' families were wasted in Nepal with smallpox.

"I think your Grandma Annie knows the key to the puzzle...I gotta' go, ...they's here...with his Emerald Dragon...find her, Buddy...she needs to know I always loved her...take me home..."

Her voice indeed trailed off like she was flying away up to go over the Rim of Heaven.

Following her funeral, her solicitor read the Will and Aubrey's witness, nobody else was left to contest Rose's sanity.

Later, as snow fell in fluffy flakes, I waited for her cremation. After helping Aubrey move into Rose's home, I moved the motorcycle where I could get repairs done on

Bryan's dust-covered Matchless 500.

I returned to Denton, Texas for a cup and crowd of friends at Amy and Joey's Jupiter House Coffee Shop on the east side of Town Square. The morning coffee clan flocked around the deep-British-green antique treasured 1957 Matchless 500.

Dave Will, Heath, Jim, Jimmy, Joe Powell, Louie, Mike, Ron, Stephen and Shakey-cup John, most divorced, each and everyone; AA members, disabled 'Nam vets, tunnel rats, retired snipers, or Ex-DEA agents, and a German Shepherd named Harley. With a Ron Paul rally at the Courthouse, they had all the available parking spaces filled up like a motorcycle showroom and political primary.

Camaraderie is a great place for young and old divorced men to lick their wounds. Of course, women filing in and out of the coffee shop will forever remain an unprescribed, sweet visual remedy; like; Amy, Cassandra, Elizabeth, Lorena, Meredith, Pam, and Ms. Kellie LeFray.

After firm handshakes and a few hugs from several survivors and sweethearts, I said, "What's better news of hometown than over the rim of a full coffee cup?"

Jim Griffin reported, "Charlie died."

"Which one? The wheelchair can-man, or Charlie from New Mexico's Film Commissioner?"

"I stand corrected. Charles Krantz."

"That's the best bad news I've heard. He already spent his time in his wheelchair from hell." I reflected, "Prisoners get better equipment than law-abiders. He used to re-break his, 'skin-and-bone,' hips every time he stood up from his used 'Cadillac' to dig through trashcans."

David Ater added, "Dietrich was 86'ed for bumming cigarettes, money and coffee. He came out one morning without his meds and lost control after two-cup Mike wouldn't give him a smoke."

Jim Griffin added, "He's going to have his parole revoked if he goes on a rampage."

"Yeah," we pretty much all agreed, "I can only hope no one gets hurt or killed."

We all understood his hard-time prison art of persuasion; he was pretty much like a friendly, tail-waggin' Pitbull until we cut off his free supply of smokes.

I reminisced a couple seconds, "His heart isn't visibly strangled with barbed-wire-bigotry but it's sad that he'll likely lose his parole over panhandling."

"Buddy," Jim pointed out, "He'll lose his parole because of assault with intent to kill."

"Then it's me who stands corrected. Where's the four-man poker club?"

Ron spoke up this article of police-blotter information, "They harvested their home-grown and were picked off one by one as they left their hot-house."

Jim Griffin nodded his head from already pulling up the police report at his barbershop.

"How much were they carrying?" I knew they never dealt with risk and dealers. They never sold any to others. Their crop was purely personal use, but they made a poor choice. Each one had a beautiful wife and a couple kids.

Jim filled in the arrest information: "Over four ounces,

less than five pounds."

"Cripes! That's a felony charge."

"Well, the indictments probably won't come down till just before a year is up," said Jim.

Crystal, apt to surely vote for Hillary, shook her head. Crystal's sister was one of the men's wives. "They used a whole S.W.A.T. team, teargas and cluster bombs to throw into one's home. It was fortunate that Pam and the girls were visiting relatives in Colorado."

I certainly had to agree with that, still, they chose to break a law and that choice included the consequences for their freedom.

"I'm glad I missed it all. Dietrich would probably have singled me out and I'd be his to blame. As for the jail-birds, they allow poker clubs in federal prisons."

Jimmy used to be a tunnel rat and explosives expert in Vietnam. He asked, "You've missed a lot of morning business meetings. Where the hell have you been and when or how did you find the green dragon?"

While thinking I'd been hearing a lot about Green Dragons, I knew Jimmy was a professional cycle racer and went most places over a hundred miles per hour. I explained recent travel news to which I added, "I'm planning a trip up to Eastern Washington…under the speed limit."

Jimmy smiled and Mike Boodt, Jim Griffin too, suggested, "Buddy, it's still winter; store your Matchless and fly, drive or both."

"Y'all are probably right. I even thought of dragging my butt on a Greyhound; I just don't think I'll try to rent a car and drive it with fuel costs being so high."

Louie Apple used to drive moving vans. Older, retired, voting for Huckleberry, he suggested, "You can Amtrak to Elko, Nevada. You told me that's where you worked once. There, you might think about buying a good pickup and going north through the scenery along the Columbia River headwaters until you come to Wenatchee. I know you'd love the scenery. The only wild patch to drive across is through the Owyhee Indian Reservation."

I couldn't have felt more in agreement. I always shared my monthly issue of *Country* with Louie Apple. He finished his suggestion with, "But you gotta have a steak at the Star Cafe."

"Well, damnation, this has been the most news I've heard, unless Courts Griner found his backyard Bigfoot. Unless there's more news of girlfriends and golf scores, I guess today's meeting is adjourned."

Pretty much everyone laughed, left for work or bought refills. The Jupiter House owners, Joey and Amy, said, "Have a safe trip, but be sure to make it back for our Jazz Festival weekend."

CHAPTER TWO

With Grandma Rose by my side within a silvery etched and inlaid urn, I flew out of DFW up to Denver, then rode rails through Ogden, Utah to Elko, Nevada, just for a famed steak from the Star Restaurant.

On the way out, I slid a Liberty dime down the throat of a one armed bandit and won enough to replace my gaucho boots with a pair of red and black Noconas. I also bought a 300 Savage, a couple handguns, ammo, a new duster, a pair of Bucks' Gloves and a, "Brindle" leather hat, both hand sewn. I bid my last $600.00, for a faded, emerald green, Forest Service ¾ ton pickup.

Luck would have it no other way. Granny Rose would be riding home on the front seat of an emerald dragon.

Strapping in four extra tires on wheels and the same number of GI gas cans behind the truck's tool bin, I opened my last carton of Skydancer cigarettes and drove the rest of the way from Elko, Nevada, the morning a 6.3 earthquake rattled night-long gamblers, whores and residents awake.

I turned off my cellphone, gave up shaving, named my truck "Liberty," and drove west through the huge, gold mining operations that started it all back in 1964.

I'd worked U.S. Forest Service in the Ruby Mountains to the southeast of Elko. The story of the Maggie Creek gold mine came from the early 60's, when a prospector sold his claim for $10,000.00 to Newmont Mining Company. After Bechtel Corporation finished a processing plant and smelter,

Newmont banked a total of $10,000,000.00 in gold back when the stuff was $40.00 an ounce.

Newmont was also the big, but obscure money name in Afghanistan's gold mining operations similar to Maggie Creek north of Carlin, Nevada. Those tunnels and roads didn't build themselves.

At Carlin, I turned almost straight north past more mining companies. An enormous new tax base allowed growth of sprawling suburban developments.

Past Bing Crosby's ranch, I jammed four gears onward 'round Wild Horse Reservoir. Liberty and I wound up and down along the north banks of the Owyhee River's course to join the Columbia River.

Louie was right; the scenery had not been boring, although some folks might think it so. Northern slopes of these mountains are covered in forests of Silver Fir. Only the southern flanks of mountains appear barren from intense sunburn.

"Bam…Whoot…whoot…whooot…toot," my front right tire blew out. Almost losing control, I hit a culvert collar of crumbled concrete, which'd once had a warning marker but long since had been sheared off and grown over with weeds.

Lucky for a level fisherman's side road, I got out to swap my first spare tire. Its wheel rim was wasted from the impact on the hidden curb. The tire'd been ripped off. Leaving it to mark the signless culvert, I had time to piss on it.

I glanced around at the distant scenery. Besides the sound of my puddle, the landscape wasn't much different than Uzbekistan or Afghanistan. It was barren enough, except for sounds from a stationary flying hawk above the soft riffles of a streambed. Only yellow and black marked Meadowlarks, or black and white Magpies flitted from one clump of sagebrush to another.

I heard something scurry into a nearby bush; maybe it was a rodent. Focusing with a totally broad view, I caught a small movement. Every, late-snow-covered sagebrush seemed to shelter at least a pair of furry balls with cottontail ears.

I finished, zipped up and stretched cramps out of my legs. I didn't resist the temptation to warm up my pistols and flip a few yards of fly fishing line to provide myself with a savory breakfast and lunch of roasted rarebit, or fresh caught trout.

Out of the blue like a guitar strumming, singing songbird, I heard, "Nice shot. Good trout."

I spun around with my fishing pole in one hand and my pistol in the other. I nearly had to re-swallow my heart. Simply standing in everything found of old clothes and shoes, with a battered, hand-me-down Gibson, was a loco-looking Indian with the longest, blackest, uncut hair and ice blue eyes I'd ever looked into.

Everything went silent. I remained still, like in a spell. It seemed the world stopped turning until he said, while tracing his finger across an imagined Army nametag, "'Name's, Singer, we served together in Uzbek."

I felt suddenly unbound, "You used to say, 'If God can do it once, he can send us back twice.'"

Singer added, "My God's name is, 'Gambler,' with a surprise ace always up his sleeve. You're Buddy, yeah, 'Butts' Morgan."

I marveled at crossing paths twice in life, so far away from others and on both sides of the world. After a single hand shake pump like swinging a dry piece of dead sagebrush, I invited, "Well, are you going to stare or set down with me for food?"

Singer added, "If you cook it first." Stooping to half kneel, he gathered together what's dry and near before raising his palms up for approval of the fastest cooking fire I've ever recalled.

After cutting off the trout-heads, and skinning the rabbits' hide, I skewered them to prop over his smokeless fire.

Poppin' the rabbit's head and innards on the coals, Singer said, "Thanks for offering me some of your food, but I'll pay you this for a ride north to Wenatchee." Singer dug down in his pocket and flipped me a gold nugget the size of a peach pit.

"Singer, this is most likely worth more than everything I've got here."

"No problem, Butts. What's worth more than friends? Worth is darned overrated. I'm a Digger Indian. I grew up in this back yard. If you walk all over it, you'll find a pocket full of nuggets. But, these things are only worth the hole it'll make in your pocket. There have been times in years gone by when a wild cantaloupe, pinion nuts and rabbit fur blankets are worth more. Right now, this fire is worth everything. I do have a cellphone, though."

Laughing with the appearance of the worldly in this man's back pocket, I thought, "Singer was right," even though his fire wasn't bigger'n my hat, it was enough for our dinner.

I stuffed my precious nugget deep in my Wranglers pocket. I didn't expect he'd eat everything from the rabbit's insides plus the head, until he spit out its tiny teeth. He didn't touch the fish.

He reminded me of the old west stories of a past famed gunfighter, Porter Rockwell. That man's granddaughter had told of selling a rabbit's leftovers to a Digger Indian for a nickel.

Continuing on, we sang to range radio station tunes, while Liberty's gears whined away the hours in harmony. We crossed Owyhee Indian Reservation along dusty gravel roads with no speed limits. All night and into the next morning, after two more flats, we finally turned Liberty onto paved highways across corners of Idaho and Oregon into far eastern Washington State.

After two early morning naps and brunch in Richland, the rest of our journey was sunshine through Singer's side window. We passed Moses Lake then turned west in Grant's Orchards.

We arrived in apple country and turned north again and wove along the communities of the drier eastern Cascade Mountains.

Arriving in the city of Wenatchee, Singer helped put new tubes in the remaining flats and filled my fuel tanks. Since we'd shared food, beside hearing his life story since our last meeting, the only words he'd said besides singing lyrics was, "Call if you need help."

We shook hands, even hugged like lost brothers. He left a scribbled phone number. Before I could archive it in my cellphone's address book and look up, he'd just disappeared.

Thinking, "I could have left half my remaining Skydancers for him," seemed ridiculous; he was simply gone.

I continued on through Leavenworth on Highway 2 and slowed at Coles' Corner. I felt drawn to a road sign for a café and pulled into a place called the Blue Ox. I gingerly parked Liberty between 18-wheel logging rigs. Those trailers were loaded with one or two cut sections of trees to be milled into lumber far from their previous life and forests. I mean, these were huge pieces of trees.

Since the eruption of Mt. St. Helens to the south, many old first-growth forests were opened up to loggers, rather than be lost in a future eruption of Mt. Rainier, to the southwest, Mt Baker, to the north, or Mt. Hood in Oregon.

Little Annapurna is in the Alpine Meadow Wilderness, east of Mt. Daniel. If Rainier erupted, Little Annapurna could be spared the devastation likes of what Mt. St. Helens did to Spirit Lake and Ike Truman's Resort, but only prophets tell the future.

Leaving Liberty, with one hand holding my hat down tight on my noggin and my duster tails blowing more like sails of ships, I braced dry gusts of strong evening wind. Once inside, I opened the second inner door; the sound of jukebox songs mixed with the smell of snoose, sawdust, sweat, diesel oil, hot black coffee and sizzling steaks. The aroma of fresh baked hot-rolls and homemade pie made it all fit together better.

Hanging up my brindle and black duster, I scanned the interior and Saturday night folks who were there. The only waitress was busy with platters for a large group of large men. The man cooking behind the counter spoke out a cordial greeting for foreign strangers and said, "There's the coffee cups and java; pour your own brand of whiskey, though." He meant it. In a cabinet, several brands of fifths were tucked next to the brewing coffee urns.

One of the separated loggers snubbed out a cigar butt after spittin' in the ashtray near my hand. He eyed my hat and duster and looked down at my boots with a mocking sneer as he got up to leave.

I half expected him to spit out trouble or mess with my hat and duster but ignored it, yet I noticed, other than his frying-pan-sized rodeo belt buckle, his boots were Justin Ropers.

He spiked a battered stainless thermos of black coffee with an extra chug of Black Label Jack Daniels then cracked open a new can of Copenhagen in which he sprinkled cayenne pepper before he trickled a couple drops more of Black Jack.

Shortly, the busy little waitress came up to the counter where I'd parked my tired butt on a cushioned, hand-hewn stool. As I shucked my gloves, she scowled, muttered some epithet, "Motherless Bastard!"

She grabbed away my ashtray and slung it bulls-eyed into the trash, rather than clean it. She replaced another for the first flicks off my Skydancer, which I'd lit. Guessing she was about as tall as my duster, she leaned way over the counter to also glance down at my red and black size 13's and asked, "You want the special this evening?"

I remembered the size of her full platters and asked, "If that's the special, I wouldn't have room for one corner of it? I forgot to order dessert at Star's in Elko, I'd settle for a piece of that apple pie and a scoop of vanilla ice cream, though."

"Elko's best steak house, huh? Got'cha," was all she replied as if the book of my life and map of my road had just been read.

She slid a warmly loaded, quarter piece of apple pie a-la-mode toward me. When she'd leaned over the counter to look at my boots, I'd seen enough fullness pressed inside her waitress blouse to be pleased. My glance at her hands told me she wasn't wearing a wedding ring, so I spoke, "Thanks, Miss."

Smiling with her own review of where my eyes were drawn, she added, "Thanks accepted. I saw after pulling off those nice gloves, that you're not wearing a ring, either."

"Married once, divorced once."

She continued as a mild uncomfortable blush rose up my two-day old, unshaved rusty scruff then stated rather than asked, "You be the young man Annie's waiting to see."

"Annie," I answered with disbelief?

"Yep, your Great Grandma, Annie Cole; she has the gift of dreams. From what she's described, it's all over the shape of your face."

I tendered my hand and offered my name, "Buddy Morgan, just came back from active service."

She empathized, "Lots have changed but lots more...not."

Not only was I enjoying her rare, tiny ringlets of blonde-haired beauty, I was surprised; amazed could be the word for the melody in her voice. I felt I'd better answer in true words, "Can't say you're wrong. Don't think I'd like to say so, but I sure need to know how to get up to Annie's place."

"'Name's Maggie Cole. Annie's my great-aunt."

She gave me a strong handshake then volunteered, "Stick around. I'll lead you to her home as soon as I'm off my shift."

Grabbing a new hot pot of coffee in one hand and Jack Daniels in the other, she hurried off to the group of loggers. One by one, their heads turned to check me out.

Before I finished the best pie I'd forked over my tongue, the "band of brothers" got up to leave. Each one shared a greeting or handshake reserved only for live, returned veterans before setting their dinged, bent hard-hats and sturdy logger boots in the direction of their parked rigs.

Maggie spoke up after the last one left, "They're your best friends if you're good enough kin for Aunt Annie calling you to come visit. She's raised, schooled or tanned hides of every one of those fellers," adding, "…no one sharpens cutting tools better than Aunt Annie."

I asked, "Who's the other guy who left earlier?"

Maggie answered with a covered up tone. "That's Bristol. He knows trees and works hard but expects me to be his woman like some kind of leash pet."

"I don't like him. Do you know if he's from Texas?"

Maggie agreed first, "Good! Then that makes one more than all the rest of us; but Texan, I don't know. Be careful. Watch your rear view mirror if he's behind you and stay out of his way if he's coming downhill in front of you."

"Done, Maggie."

Turning toward the burly cook, Maggie stated matter-of-factly, "Daddy Red, I'll be home after I get Buddy up to Annie's."

All six-foot-six, 300-plus pounds of "Daddy Red," came out from behind the kitchen order window, wiped wet and grease on his apron then swallowed my hand in his vise-like grip.

"Come see us soon. 'Don't get 'nuf news of Annie since she had a bout of dizzy spells."

"Yes sir."

He made no glance or mention of my "devil-be-damned" boots. He simply turned away after flipping off the, "Open" sign and went back to finish scrubbing his grill clean of the nights' rendering.

Maggie finished folding up tips as I felt the necessity of cleaning my plate of apple pie a-la-mode. She flipped off the jukebox in the middle of a Johnny Cash singing slower and lower, "…hotter than a pepper sprout…"

She hung up her apron before grabbing her warm Mack under arm to sit close beside me, like a long, lost sister.

I scolded my thoughts about how pretty she was and me just a stranger. I began to fish out money to pay.

She playfully hugged my elbow with a little shove, "Already done, Buddy."

She must have put rocks in her overcoat pockets to stay on the ground after leaving the café. Half shouting over the wind she instructed, "Next stop is the Valley of the Dragons. Don't follow too close, our wind gusts can often reach 100 miles an hour and known to set a whole tree down across the road. Most log drivers are down the mountain now, keep up, keep behind and keep right. Don't be surprised if you see a bear or Bigfoot."

While we pulled out of the parking lot onto the highway, I thought, perplexed: "But Annie didn't call me!"

CHAPTER THREE

Maggie knew her roads. I hung on tight to Granny Rose's urn of ashes. I faulted a few curves and prayed thanks for fishtailing with rear-wheel drive. A heavy steel plate on the truck bed and load of extra tires and fuel cans, helped weigh matters down.

Most of the roads skirted shear drop-offs. Along the birms, snow banks still gathered at the bases of what looked like upended dragon scales.

Hardly a half hour later, her taillights showed brightly through the higher mountains' fine dust. The lower elevation winds were no slower, being so close to home up here.

Arriving at what first looked like a dead-end scenic lookout, she was by my cab before I could get out my front door. "Your booty's safe here. Grab what you'll need, I'll help pack what you can't tote. We've got a little hike up to Annie's hanging valley meadow."

I locked my larger duffel full in the toolbox, put one pistol in my neckline holster and necessities in my Army Ranger pack. After I pulled its strap over my head and shoulder, I tucked Granny Rose snugly inside my black duster pocket.

Maggie checked her .357-magnum loads and then pulled out an automatic, .28-caliber. She fired off one shot. Upon seeing my tote bag's insignia, she respectfully apprised, "Didn't know you were a Ranger."

While her shot finished echoing around some canyon

walls with the songs of the wind, I answered, "Didn't know I was either, until I survived long enough to get labeled so. Seer training's not the same as Seals. I started out as a Naval Air, language cryptographer until someone saw me mark a twelve hundred yard kill shot with a friend at Ft. Benning, Georgia, so I was a sniper for the last five and a half of ten mixed service years. I was stationed in Uzbekistan, first. I froze off three toes, then went to Afghanistan before ending up blowing out my knee in a Baghdad parachute jump as a team leader for six other snipers."

"How many languages?"

I had no problem with telling her, but tried to do it without sounding like a braggart, "Enough."

As we began walking a faint, snow-covered trail, we basically disappeared between widely spaced vertical slabs. I marveled at these formations of upended stone segments. I asked, "These aren't granite, what is it called?"

Maggie answered as I stroked one with my hand, "Geologists call them slicum scales; it's a form of chrome-bearing ore.

"Kinda looks and feels like slippery dragon scales too?"

She didn't let her curiosity loose of my language training, "Which ones?"

Giving up easy enough, I rattled off a list: "Arabic, after a year at the Monterrey, California, Defense Language Institute. Otherwise, I picked up enough French, German, Italian, and Spanish while my mother's travels kept me in Europe during the late sixties and seventies. When Mom moved to Southern Brazil, I learned Portuguese. The Hebrew, Hindi, Russian, Chinese and a fair mix of regional combinations, I picked up during her travels across Southern Asia."

"Damnation, Buddy! You might be a hell of a good time at next week's Polka Night."

Her smile took my attention from the side of the trail and I slipped and got slapped in the shoulder with a Devil's Club. I hadn't forgotten how her well-shaped curves fit warmly inside her bulky Mac.

"If you'd look where you're going instead of thinking about my ass…" She left her words unfinished, but with a small smile beneath her twinkling eyes.

"I wasn't thinking of just your rear bumper. You've got a couple other moderately sized fenders on my mind."

"Oh! Well let me tailgate behind you for the rest of the way."

"There's not much to see inside a duster," I chuckled.

Maggie laughed back, "From what I saw in the Blue Ox, I'd have to ask, 'Do you even have an ass at all'?"

With that said, we shut up and followed the pale outline of a switchback trail under the shadows of a full moon comin' up. A quarter mile of windblown zigzags through sheltered timber and dragon scales passed too quickly. I heard the sound of a waterfall to my left before stepping around a steep ledge. The wall of stone, timber and brush gave way to an opening into a side canyon.

I'd have never guessed it was there from the lookout where we'd parked our trucks. Almost suddenly, the winds were calm. I thought, "'Guess we're all home."

Before my eyes, a terraced hillside of herbs and berries sloped away. Annie's Valley of the Dragons opened into a silvery verdant meadow surrounded by a fruit tree orchard.

Her home was clustered within a barn, stables, and out buildings close by her beautiful cottage in the distance.

The hanging valley was just this side of a sheer drop-off, about eight hundred feet of drop-off. Below higher barren, shear, mountain slopes, the entire cirque looked to be surrounded with huge first growth monarchs of Fir. Deer and elk bolted away as we appeared. They had about a mile of cover to disappear within the back of the valley.

A noisy cackle of Guinea hens erupted. With Maggie coming up to be in the lead, I heard the sound of a distant hammer on an old .58 caliber flintlock ear back. She called out, "Annie, it's Maggie. I've got Buddy with me…your great grandson."

The source of the sound of a hammer's release was a great relief. Then, she lit a lantern to show where she was.

Little Annapurna's lower larch and fir forests framed the bright spot around her as she stood on the upper cottage porch.

I turned to thank Maggie, but she'd just disappeared along the same footsteps we'd made in the snow.

Behind my puzzled look, Great Granny Annie's melodic voice rang like a gentle wind-chime, as well as the precise diction of an aged English teacher, "Do not be hurt, nor worried, she'll let us know when she makes it to her truck."

She lifted her storm lantern and said, "Come on up, son."

In the dim light, I ascending her first floor stairs and followed inside her home. She hung my Army Ranger tote over a spike of Elk antlers underneath "Bess."

She explained, "Bess, my 1796 Brown Bess musket."

I answered, ".58 caliber...I've heard 'em before in Uzbekistan," I let my eyes adjust to the single, lantern-lit surroundings.

Annie eyed me and poked over a fireplace log before she added another piece of knothole for brightness. The years of savory smoke had darkened most of the walls, even though they'd once been whitewashed, perhaps several times.

I was about to extend the urn with Lorena's ashes to her Mom, when a distant pistol shot made me flinch around to face the door. Another shot followed. I danged near dropped Grandma Lorena all over the truncheon floor planks.

Eyeing the decorative ceramic urn, Annie whispered about Maggie, "She's OK; that's our sign for goodbye," then she tenderly hugged Lorena Rose's remains to her bosom.

Speaking of Rose's ashes, tears dampened the wrinkles beside her pale blue eyes, "She was my best; took off with a no-good logger, though. They settled in Arkansas before he deserted her 'n' a baby boy. He never married her to give a proper name to their son, so she gave her boy our last name."

While she placed the urn on an upper shelf of a magnificently filled bookcase, I told her the rest of Rose's story and thought Annie was going to laugh to death, except, she caught her hands up to her throat when she heard about her husband and brother-in-law.

While she cried quietly, I glanced around. I recalled how from the outside, the look of her home was something like a Hansel and Gretel gingerbread house. Hand-cut and sculptured, multi-colored shake-shingles extended from her metal rooftop and second floor gables down each wall to protect the top and first floor of her dwelling.

Annie's front door opened onto a wide porch level with the top of winter snows; another bottom layer of the cottage's walls were built from hexagonal basaltic chunks. Her ground floor doorways only opened in late spring and summer after snows had thawed away to pine needles of ancient fir and larkspur.

Her upper third floor was odd, in a simple kind of way. She used it for an observatory. I thought, "Nice place to pick off whiskers on kittens in any direction." Last, she showed me to an upstairs loft with a bunk beside the warm stones of the upper chimney. "Your slop jar is under the bed; God be praised I get to meet you." She hugged me strong and kissed my cheek, "Sleep well."

Sleep well, I did, except when wet snow slid off metal roof panels and woke me up before daylight. In the morning, I felt like 150 years had been erased. She had plenty for me to help do and did a lot more than I thought was needful. My clothes were scrubbed and neatly pressed before I woke up.

If I wasn't fully awake, before I'd hurried to the outhouse with a full plumbing system, I was wide awake from the meadows' crisp morning air. I knelt down by the shoreline and smoked a couple cigarettes. I scanned in every direction to get a map started in my mind.

Beside another small structure, there was a small swimming hole of sorts just upstream from the outhouse. I was surprised to discover, "It's a sauna."

Annie even had fire ready in its steam room before a quick streaking plunge in the icy water. It sure made me ready for a new day.

I took a seat in her warm kitchen, at the end of a table. Solid and simple, it could serve a fair size Thanksgiving or family reunion dinner. With Annie's first served platter, we sat together and asked a blessing on our food and needs of the day.

Tucking on the napkin she'd provided, I delivered fork after hungry forkfuls of grilled, glazed ham and butter-fried eggs 'n' wild mushrooms.

"Ma'am, that's the finest ham steaks I remember ever eating."

While she toasted homemade bread slices over her Matheson's Wood Burning Stove's range, she answered, "Good, call me Annie; it's not ham, it's bear."

Then, a plate of hot toast was set beside me to smother in more rich butter and fresh berry jam, …and that was before griddlecakes, homemade syrup and apple pie.

For six days and nearly all of six nights long, Annie made me at home, warm and fed better than my mother, Navy, Army or ex-wife thought possible, or I felt was possible for a ninety-nine-year-old great-grandmother.

Her stove could heat four ironing plates off a tray that ran along the stove's back. Its' warming oven, or as she called it, "My pie oven," was elevated about her shoulder level. A copper, five-gallon tank was set above her pie oven. Vented off the stove's heat, it gave all her hot water needs through a simple spigot.

Our first night after a full workday of learning how to correctly sharpen tools, she asked questions of nearly all my life.

I related how, "Before I was born, my mom took a job as an intelligence operative after my father had tried to beat her into a miscarriage. She'd refused to have an abortion."

Annie responded, "Bad seed from your daddy skips a generation now and then. I don't see it in you."

I also told how I spent my early childhood every summer at my mom's Arkansas parents'. While there, I saw my Dad for only a week of each year until news came from the Department of the Army that he'd been killed in El Salvador.

"After graduating High School, I enlisted for the Navy Cryptographer's School. By the time I was scooped out of submarines and Seer trained for Naval Air, I was away from home on top secret deployments for at least three months at a time."

After confessing. "I simply left my only marriage from my first wife when she had also taken up with a lady and a lot of drugs. Divorce was simple but its still like having an arm cut off.

"My next re-enlistment followed an accurate shooting incident, which transferred me into Ft. Benning, Georgia for Army Ranger's Sniper Training."

Annie fidgeted with my gizmos. Our topic of conversation stopped until she put it to rest. "Foolish girls are what St. Paul called them. It was good for you to just go away. The Good Book says, 'Empty the net and start over'."

Our first conversation was enough, if not too much, for starters. We went to bed. I struggled with recalled good and bad memories, but soon didn't hear another thing until sunshine and late spring snowflakes hit the upstairs, loft windows.

During breakfast, I asked her permission to clear a road for a driveway into her place. She agreed saying, "Actually the path used to be a wagon road; follow it as best possible. There's lots of old tools in the workshop, which Sam and Tex used to do their fix-up-jobs."

After breakfast dishes were taken care of, I walked with Annie to her husband's shop. "I never use it much. Everything I need for sharpening jobs are in my sewing room."

All total, Sam's workshop was a sturdy structure about 200 square feet. To either side of the front door, a jobs-bench extended around two of the sunny sides of the structure.

Annie showed me how to raise the top four feet of three wall panels into comfortable breezeway openings and to let in daylight. She simply returned towards her home. "Dinner's at sundown."

While smoking another Skydancer, I saw every sort of blacksmith, saddle, harness, carpentry or mechanic and plumbing tools. Separated, yet nearby Annie's barn and stables for the milk cows and horses, the yard anvil, hoists and hay derricks filled up space between the coops for ducks, geese and chickens.

Annie kept cats, but not dogs. Her guinea hens raised all the alarm necessary of visitors, be they friends or strangers. Her dozen horses and five milk cows would fare well in the fenced-off verdant pastures full of white milkweed fluffs, tall yellow columbine, blue lupine and whatever kind of red wildflowers, of which I'd like to learn all the names.

For the next ten days as a road building engineer, the weather teeter-tottered, like a drunk Irishman; Winter, and Spring, and Summer, and back again.

At Annie's little observatory in her upper balcony, she told me, "I cannot say much about global warming; I know more about Earth crossing the Solar Plane around 2012."

While I was fascinated with all the antique tools in Sam's old workshop, during evenings, Annie was fascinated with my gadgets and computer gimmicks. It sure made recording easier. I'd never have wanted to forget her beautiful voice, sorta like Swiss Mountain folks speak with singing.

On Friday night of my second week, my green dragon was parked in a little circle up beside her front yard's picket gate. Weather was clear and warm enough to make mud-pie ice cream.

After dinner, Annie sat in her porch rocker while I eased onto the middle of a latticed swinging bench. While sipping coffee we listened. She said of the winds, "They're coming home to bed."

I fidgeted in my pocket, pulled out my last Skydancer and asked, "Annie, do you mind…?"

She produced a corncob hotbox and thumb-struck a blue-tip. "You're welcome to smoke yours if you don't mind me smoking my own brand."

I knew that smell from past experiences but offered no comment.

She read my mind, "Fountain of youth and best asthma medicine from the Indians' pharmacy."

That's when we heard a single pistol shot. Annie smiled, then stated, "Saw you flinch, but felt your heart skip a beat, too. That'll be Maggie coming to visit."

"Yep, it was a warmed up skip of a heartbeat," I smiled back. Guinea hens set off their cackling alarm. Then, she was there again, in her four-wheel rig. She parked with a big smiling, "Wahoo!" as she jumped out of her truck and skipped easily to the garden gate. Even in sturdy logger boots, her long legs and wide hips were all the right kind of Gods' architecture of a woman's legs.

Looking back and forth between Maggie and me, Annie read us like a pair of book covers just waiting to be bound around a life-long story.

⚜ CHAPTER FOUR ⚜

Before Maggie opened up the picket gate, Annie had me blushing with little taunting dares. When she stepped up onto the porch, we were both immediately sobered to see a mouse-sized reddish-purple bruise under Maggie's left eye.

As Maggie expressed speechless hand and arm movements about the new driveway, Annie breathed a deep sigh and rather than asking for an explanation let loose one, "Ha-ha," as she tenderly stroked a mothers' healing caress, "I guess I know what Bristol's face looks like; but, which end of the axe handle did you use?"

Maggie's smile left a bit of imagination, or future consideration. Simply put, silence was a golden answer but I yearned to deliver my own form of retribution. I was already standing up to let Maggie have a seat on Annie's porch swing.

"You've got a new road, I love it! Oh, thanks." She latched hold of my hand, tugged me down and kissed me on about a two-week old growth of rusty red beard repeating again, "Its great, I looovvveee it!"

Expecting neither, exclamations or movement, the warmth of her closeness cleared the stage for my little digital recorders' production.

I played back Lorena's voice for Granny Annie and Maggie. We laughed again at the confession about her no-good husband but Annie began to cry while hearing her last daughters' words about the "Emerald dragon."

This time, Maggie sat forward, bent over and rested her cheek on my knee and smiled up at Annie with an expression full of empathy.

While I massaged Maggie's neck and back, like I'd done so for years, my short recording finished.

As Annie pointed with explanation of Lorena's narrative, I switched on the record mode again. "Little Annapurna is that mountains' name. These Washington State's Northern Cascades, which are east of volcanoes, have a geology from the bottom side of Earth's mantle"

I realized seeing it before on Roses' door at the rest home as Annie sipped tiny puffs from her pipe's bowl.

"This mountain bears a resemblance to the daughter of Shagarmatha. The British renamed, 'Mother of all Mountains,' Mt. Everest. Immediately west of Everest is she who is named Annapurna; K-2 is the name on modern maps."

"Lorena Annapurna was also the name of the seventh wife of my legendary grandfather, Tiex Buda. My grandmother's father was the most feared of Ghurkha Tribal Kings, and a direct descendant of the Black Goat Mountain child."

"Lorena Annapurna's father had tried nine times to sire an heir to his kingdom and son to his name.

I slid in a few quick words, "Does Annapurna translate close enough to Anna-mamma?"

Annie continued, "I like that, but it's more like, 'Anna's Tit.'" We all laughed as Annie went on, "She was the youngest and most unruly of his nine daughters; the most beautiful of the kings' fearsome family. All were skilled with swords or bullets, but Anna-mamma had even bested her fathers' finest warriors, in games of swords, though."

Annapurna's story passed on to me was, "My father joked, 'your mother must have eaten a Mongoose on the night you were conceived.' You're beautiful as a rosebud, but your pretty hide's covered in thorns."

"To Lorena Annapurna, the world of men and all their rules for women were something to be bested if not ignored."

Breaking off from her narrative, Annie said, "Oh Maggie, I'm getting forgetful. I didn't get you a cup."

Annie didn't creak or rise with a squeak before Maggie said, "I know where they are."

She fetched three tin cups in one hand; her other palm lovingly wrapped a homebrew of Wake Water.

Annie put away her pipe, poured and raised a tin cup toast "…Schlog, after schlog, here's a grog to Lorena Rose and all the best of the men she rests with…no sippers allowed on the first cup."

Maggie must have had practice with this brand of Annie's berry brandy. I didn't want to make a mistake of inhaling before I swallowed.

Three chugs slapped down all emptied tin cups to sound like one.

On a whim, I flicked my Zippo and its flame went, 'Poof!' with a blue blaze into the cup. I commented hoarsely, "I thought so!"

Maggie giggled and poured the next round while Annie continued where she'd left off. Maggie snuggled closer to the heartbeat side of me.

"Many ages ago, the legendary Black Goat mountain-child was found being suckled on milk of a lost she-goat. He was named Narayan Shah and became the first Ghurka King. Narayan Shah was also the name of Lorena Annapurna's father.

"Young men, when at the age of manhood, took the perilous journey of twenty-eight days into the far western ranges of the Black Goat Kings' legendary Crystal Mountain. Once there, young men purified themselves by ritually circling the Sacred Mountain an auspicious number of nine times. Cleansed men then proceeded to the headwaters of the Bramhaputra River, called Tamchok Khambab.

"It means 'out of the horse's mouth'. Kiangs are the name of the regal, hardy Asian horses, which live deep within this secret and sacred place whose high, Rim of Heaven meadow sands are made of cats-eyes and emeralds.

"If a young man survived leopards called, Snow Lions, or Yeti attacks, he entered this sacred and holy ground through treacherous ice caves. Usually, a glacier seals the entrance.

"Once within the Cave of Dragons, the Goddess of the Mountain would then bless the young male initiate. He had to retrieve his gift from the bottom of icy pools. These fabulous jewels are known as 'Dragons' Eyes'. Each kind of precious gemstone bequeathed special keys and priesthood powers to be desired and possessed.

"Other than the breastplate of twelve stones, known as the Urim and Thummin, last worn by High Priests of Ancient Israel, no one else had been bequeathed the pairs of the last six known dragon eyes.

"Rarely did a young man get a gift of any jewel; he'd at least secure casting slabs, with which to molten their Khukris, the famed swords of the Ghurkha warriors. With these slabs, the endowment included the special honing stones with which to sharpen their weapons."

With Annie's pause again to give a little burp, Maggie and me were sipping into our third tin cup full as Annie paused to whistle down the last of her second cup.

Maggie raised a toast this time to the full moon. Annie coughed out softly a tiny wheeze, "That's my wake limit, Lorena!"

I was well buzzed after my third cup was emptied. Maggie sat up again and stretched her arm around my back and nudged me forward for my turn at the rub club.

Annie didn't miss a thing, smiled wistfully at us as she continued with my taped transcription.

"In 1813, Nepal's new young King and his prime minister, Bhimsen Thapa, had declared war against India during the second decade of the 1800s. While traveling as young students throughout India they realized full well the British East India Company's intentions were clearly including colonization of Nepal. British intellectuals of the middle 1800s also entertained annihilation of lesser species of peoples and animals.

"The invasion by Nepal was instigated for more reasons than British officers using the Himalayan foothills as a summer retreat. There had been more than degrading behavior inflicted upon local residents, especially women; rapes, atrocities and murders had also been committed.

"Four regiments tried to enter the Katmandu Valley. Only one made it through. The other three were wiped out. The spearhead regiment was routed badly, their only surviving Commander deserted rather than to face the shame of not dying with his men.

"The man known as Tiex Buda had lost, both mother and father, as well as six first wives, children and relatives of the King."

We fell silent to consider everything we'd heard and all around us. Our sky behind Little Annapurna had gone through a super display of sunset colors. Even the full moon, like perhaps all our hearts, was still in the pink of things.

Suddenly, I flinched at a questioned thought, "I did turn the recorder back on, didn't I?"

Maggie remembered for me, "It's on."

What a relief. After I was sitting up now, Maggie tucked up her knees and sort of curled onto my lap with one palm slid discreetly between my thighs. Annie's smile was of total satisfaction. None of us had yawned, yet…Oooops!

Annie giggled before she got started again. Repeating more than Granny Rose's details, she added,

"Also, Tiex Buda was a friend of Bhimsen Thapa's nephew named Jang Bahadar. Jang later became a new prime minister in 1845.

"Tiex's father, Everest of Buda, was also protector of the King's family. Besides Tiex's schooling with the ancient Order called, Sons of Dragons, his father was an honored, royal mercenary."

"Premonition filled his father's heart when he left his son for the last time. He passed on a pendant of a leopard's tooth for his son to wear and saluted him with his sword of legend.

"That sword's hilt was of pure gold. It was passed down from fathers to sons from Iberian wars while their ancestors fought for Alexander the Great. His sword is only one treasure among hordes taken by a hand full of treacherous members of ill-fated East-India Regiments.

"Tiex Buda's father promised his sword would pass to his only son when his then child was not even strong enough to lift it or even wrap tiny fingers around the smoothly worn ivory handle.

"Everest retrieved it but was later killed, while defending immediate family members as well as the king's loved ones.

"Annapurna's husband, as said before, was commissioned to seek out and deliver retribution for atrocities committed by the fourth surviving regiment's soldiers, and protect the king's eldest son, Krough Shah.

"The Goddess named Kali is the name of a tributary pouring into the lower Bhramaputra River. Kali is known as, 'the Goddess who brings smallpox'. Every family touched by the East India companies had been visited by Kali.

"Tiex Buda's first six wives and children were among those who were defiled before being murdered by exposure to smallpox. Revenge for the death of his father and several wives with children was a multi-fold, family tragedy.

"Although retaliation festered in his heart, his commission from the King would place Karma within his loyal hands. It took him and "Crow" halfway around the world, from the foothills of the Himalayas of Asia, to the Himalayas of America.

"Prior to Tiex's Buddhist orphange schooling, he was taught by his father. Those rare times he spent as a child actually taught him nine numbers by counting his father's scars from swords, knives, bullets or arrows.

"His father told Little Tiex the lineage of their predecessors. They included makers of arms and accoutrements of wars from Eastern Europe's Buda, near Peste. Other forefathers, all mercenaries, hailed from vast histories of Germanic Hessians, Scottish Blackwatch Highlanders and British Cymeric descendants of Arimethea and Avalon's fabled Pendragon Knights and Generals.

"Anciently known Old Testament records affirmed his genealogy went back to daughters of Zedekiah brought by Jeremiah to Brittain and Iberia, and farther back to, Judah's son, Zarah, who is twin brother of Perez."

"Tiex Buda's heritage is indeed proud and illustrious, yet quiet, non-assuming and acting only with mercenary purpose.

"Noted Sons of Dragons, possessed mental and physical skills unparalleled in world history. As a child, Tiex was always picked on, looked different, too. His voice quivered with a high pitch and his hands trembled when enraged. Worst of all, he'd pee his pants.

"There was one time when he turned on his previous bullies that were picking on another smaller child named Jang Bahadur. Tiexs' actions of defense were cold, clever and calm as never before experienced. The small boy he'd protected turned out later to become Nepal's prime minister in 1845.

"A visiting Shaman from Crystal Mountain witnessed his defensive actions. He selected Tiex and for the next ten years, taught him all the Brahman and Shaman leaders of ancient wisdom and secrets.

"As I related earlier, Fate had failed the direct descendant of Narayan Shah's many attempts to sire a Ghurka King's son. When Annapurna came to her time of becoming a woman, she'd rather not submit to becoming a wife to a husband of her father, the Ghurka Kings' choosing.

"She took it upon herself to take the journey of ritual only permitted by laws for men. She trespassed her womanhood and secretly left for the sacred place of male endowments.

"Anna-mamma's disappearance was a great cause for alarm. The Yeti, known in their language as the 'Bear-Man', is called a 'Dremo.' Even today, many young women's disappearances are explained as abductions by Dremos.

"Annapurna's father was heartbroken. His grief brought his gray hairs down nigh unto his deathbed.

"Only when she returns with Tiex Buda as her protector after an adventure with a great snow leopard and a befriended Dremo, does Lorena Annapurna's father find himself torn with emotions of rage and joy.

"Having already been brought down low from grief over his lost daughter, he is bound by law to sentence punishment for her actions of desecration and trespass into the Cave of Dragons.

"His judgment upon her would carry with it, a horrible and ignominious death. Instead, the King's Wise Men counseled, "Give your unruly daughter in marriage to this stranger and he will pay all his miserable life with her irascibility.

"So, she is married to Tiex Buda. Actually the done deed is a source of such humor and magnitude of joke as to choke up her old father to death by laughter. His smiling, peaceful face, looked such as only found carved on a happy Buddhist statue.

"All these tales were bound together and secreted away by Tiex and Lorena before the big fire. Lorena had tried to get those stories published, like dime novels, however, she never found an editor willing to print them. Her stories told about lives of children raised in monasteries as orphans. Other tales spoke of men who battled alongside of distant Kings and Lords as professionals for hire. Her experience of meeting Tiex Buda was one which I remember being told as a child's bedtime story."

Annie stretched, yawned and stood up slowly, certainly a bit tipsy. Or, was she having a dizzy spell with stoned vertigo? I turned off my recorder and stood up to catch her if she fell.

"I'm all right, young ones, I have to piddle and get my dreams to peaceful sleep. Maggie, come inside and help me," probably meant there were some heartfelt words to be shared.

Me, I stood to stretch my warmed thighs with my own long yawn. Before returning from around backs' little white washed outhouse, Maggie was seated alone on the porch swing.

CHAPTER FIVE

She looked dazzling. She took my breath away. She gently whispered, "The moon's going to be in full eclipse tonight."

My heart was pounding, "Let's go for a walk?"

"No lovelier time. Annie's probably already asleep. She thought we'd like to trek up to the ruins."

"Ruins?"

"Tiex and Lorena Anna-mamma's first home." As she laced her fingers between mine. She finished her last tin cup's sip and burped politely, "I know the way."

We did some staggering side-by-side steps across the yard and through the back garden gate. Dancing with turns and twirls, we tripped a couple steps while looking up at the shadows' edge begin to move across the face of the moon.

I looked down and simply bent for a purified lingering first kiss. Taking a slow deep breath, I asked, "What did Annie have to tell you?"

Leaning up on tiptoes to kiss me back with more purpose and yearning, Maggie whispered, "Well, we banked up logs in the fireplace for tonight and made stove wood ready for tomorrow morning's needs. You know, regular kitchen chores."

Oh, but did she say anything about us?

"Annie reminded me, 'It's Leap-year. Make it happen!'"

"Maggie, you do make my heart hum. I hope she meant there was a warmer and comfier place to make it happen than in melted snow puddles of the ruins for a new home we haven't built yet."

We arrived at a dark structure at the very back of the cleft of the upper falls. Spring runoff was a fierce noise and sprayed mist swirled through the air and trees laden with mosses.

"It's a waterwheel."

I answered, "Are you sure? Those upper frames look like windmill blades."

"You may be right. Perhaps it's both."

The outside windmill and paddle plates had probably once powered the gristmill inside this stone building, but they were rotted away. The two-story structure was built like a stone castle out of some Frankenstein movie poster. Rounded in the front half and squared off in the back, it looked to be sound; the four-inch thick doors were certainly sound. Their three wrought iron hinges were about ten inches wide and scrolled out into riveted bands across the entire width, which bound their huge planks together.

While saying, "Better homes have been made of windmills and places like this in worse conditions," we found one door ajar on the backside of the structure. Stepping through after a shove to sweep decades of trash, we stood within silence. "Are you scared of rats or mice?"

She drew closer to me. "No, but bats and owls give me shivers. It stinks like bears have been hibernating in here, too."

Indeed, there were little fleeing, skittering sounds; tiny shrill chirps filtered down from the upper chambers' coverings. Bat dung covered the floor. Crescent moonbeams shone down through as I did a dumb thing in the darkness.

I tripped on a toppled chair leg. Sounds from thousands of wings erupted above us and blocked out the moon glow as they fled through an upstairs open window.

Grabbing Maggie's hand as she grabbed her hair, we quickly retreated outside as black, undulating clouds of bats streamed into the night sky's dim silhouette. Laughing together with shudders, I half shouted over the waterfall's roaring, "Maggie, these wind and water systems might still be operational with a few repairs."

She shouted back, "A few repairs? Yes, but it might require a steam blaster or flood to flush the entire inner chambers clean and sterile."

I felt her hug on my arm of approval as we continued over the millponds' bridge. Stopping at the middle of its curved, Oriental arch, around the quieter, backside of the mill house, we stopped and stared up at the progress of the moon's full eclipse.

I, we, yearned for each other with mutual restraint and resolve to court this within proper limits.

Maggie said, "It reminds me of cartoon animation…it's so strange, the deep rusty-orange tone called a, 'Blood Moon.'"

I was leaning on the, yet sturdy, bridge railing with her warm backside wrapped inside my duster so we could both watch the vision before our eyes.

I said, "I'd rather name it, our 'Rose Moon.'"

She reached her hands behind her back and tucked her thumbs under my belt. Her fingers didn't have to move.

Taking in deep breaths, I whispered sweet vinegar rinsed nothings about the scent in her blond haired ringlets.

Maggie kissed me again and we both could tell our passions were beginning to race towards the rim of a waterfalls drop-off.

We stepped apart. To our left was the mountains' face and millrace. Around its corner was the falls. Ahead of us, in the old growth towering majesty of trees, the ruins topped a horizontal, higher ground shelf of natural stone. They were backed into a corner where the mountain's up-ended strata looked like a twisted, nearly vertical gargoyle's grimace. Actually, it resembled a single buttress of some European Cathedral, except it served as a corner of Tiex's palace.

Maggie turned towards me and rested her head on my shoulder with her arms hugged around me and softly stroked inside my duster up and down my back.

We left the Oriental style bridge and strolled into the grove around the ruins. Without shadows from the moon's full eclipse, a warm glow still remained on everything over, around, under or inside both our hearts.

Without saying a word, we surveyed how generations of seasons and weather had chiseled and worn away most of the timbers' burned marks of checkered charcoal. Large mats of ancient heather and blueberries filled in most of the spaces between missing walls and floorings' foundations. Golden yellow blossoms of Scotch broom stood out in patchworks like a pale colored quilt in the ruins of the palace and its courtyard.

Sleeping, closed crocuses had bloomed around long forgotten flowerbeds. Sentinel chimneys stood tall like stripped ensigns. At their bases must have been the rubble of four stories and parts of collapsed staircases. To the East, one chimney looked to be where a kitchen bakery oven joined a kettle hearth.

Near the back wall, which butted up against the cliff's base, two other chimneys jutted into the darkness. Only one showed an edge of its huge fireplace hearth's stonework. It had been exposed from decades of natures cleansing hands. Beyond it, a small grove of rhododendrons had begun to blossom. If we woke up together in tomorrow's sunrise, those blossoms would be colored in pastel, frilly pinks, purples, oranges and reds.

"Maggie, I want to clear out the rubble, sort the leftover beams and stones into stacks."

"Well, Buddy, you cleared a passable road; I've no doubt you could do all of what you put your mind to. You were a team leader once, think it out and maybe we can be a team with my brothers help, too."

Stepping within vacant spaces of jumbled jack-straw beams, laterals and poles, she sat down on the only bare corner of a ceramic-glazed hearth. With a couple sweeps of her hands, we had room to sit together, to contemplate together, and to plan out decisions together.

While thinking I could still hear a muffled roar of the waterfall, even the ground under my feet seemed to vibrate, Maggie kissed a little smile and whispered, "Buddy, whether or not I love you…Daddy Red and my brothers would skin you alive for a tablecloth if your intentions are not honorable. I'm the last; his only daughter; their only baby sister…"

I kissed her gently again with a softer hush. "Maggie, I've been looking for my history and kinfolk and I believe I've found out a lot. Annie said, 'You shouldn't forget to look for your future in your search for our past.' What I'm trying to tell you is, I've been burned once already and I'm divorced, but I want you to be my future."

I shifted off the corner of the hearth bench and knelt on one knee. Looking up at the Rose Moon, we caught hold of each other's hands as the first gleam of its light returned from the shadow of Earth's procession.

"Buddy, I love you…and yes, I am virgin. Will you marry me?"

I was caught kneeling with words still stuck in my mouth. My jaw dropped open…Yes! Well…yes…I started to laugh.

"Good, it's settled."

"But, I don't have a ring for you, I mean us…I mean…!"

"I can do without one for a…teenie little while. Remember, it's Leap year. I'll see what can be done."

I stood up and shoved my hands deep in my pockets. Suddenly I knew where the ring was coming from. I clutched Singer's nugget and my eyes sparkled.

"What?" Maggie teased.

"I have a friend."

"Buddy, you've got several friends and don't know them yet. I hope I can become the best one."

"I'm reminded of what an old Texas farmer said, 'Friends are who you can work with, fight with, and keep on working together, rather than quit'."

"That makes me feel better; I can be a fighter and I'm

not a quitter. But, let me warn you, my brothers don't quit, either."

"Oh, God, you don't mean I'll have to fight each one?"

"Yes, and maybe Daddy Red, too. They're waiting for us at the weekend Polka Party. I told Daddy, I'd get there when I get done with bringing you…"

"Well, be bringing me so I can leave a note for Annie."

"I already told her before she went to bed."

It was my turn for a playful shove. It was just enough and Maggie all but spilled over the hearthstones' edge. Seated in the dirt and old ashes, she pulled me down on top of her.

Full of joy's kind of laughter she hissed back, "God, but we're going to be sooty," then locked me into her arms.

When I came up for air, I stared at a pattern of tiles on the end of the fireplace hearth. I jumped to my knees as if struck by inspiration instead of Maggie's fired kisses.

She looked at the plates I was feeling around, "Well, I'd rather have your palms feeling those couples of me that struck your attention before. What's up?"

"Grandma Rose told me there was some kind of lock, like a puzzle on a key chain. That old wrought iron chain for the fireplace damper dangles from these tile patterns. Look, Maggie, if I'm not mistaken, these tiles are designs of numbers from the language of Nepal or India."

"Oh, Buddy, you're not serious? You are serious!"

"Look, one of nine is missing within the geometric frame." I placed my big palm and other hands' fingertips against the nearest one and shoved.

"It's sliding!"

I grunted and said with effort, "Sliding, yes, but very gritty with age and likely dirt and ashes."

Maggie stood up beside me and began to blow as much loose grit away as possible. She came away laughing and spitting with a face full of soot around her mouth, nose and eyes.

We were both giddy and traded off trying to clean out more dust. She said with more laughter, "I don't think highly of blow-jobs, but this is different."

Both getting dizzy, until we couldn't 'blow-job' anymore for cackling with laughter to tears. She said, "What about water?"

I returned, "What about berry brandy?

I thought we'd both pee our hot pants before we could stop laughing enough to catch our breath.

Stopping to try being serious for a moment, Maggie asked, "What are the numbers…which ones…for that matter, we don't know the combination?"

I naming off pictures on each tile for numbers one through eight but warned, "You could be right, but what if it's booby-trapped?"

If we had naked passions and lusty activity on our minds a few moments ago, they'd politely stood back until later. With patience and gentle persuasion, we succeeded in at least getting each one to slide freely. That left the sequence as integral as a computers' password. "Let me think this out."

Sitting down again, Maggie swiveled around on the pivot of her pretty britches and we faced each other as close as knees could flex and legs draw us close around each other's embrace.

With renewed fire of yearning, she whispered, "Think this out first."

Well, we almost did. Drawing in deep breaths I let out a tortured whisper, "You're hotter than a time-bomb!"

"Yeah, well, start the countdown to missile launch," she groaned with warning. "But, Oh! Oh! ooooh aaahh, maybe that's it."

"Cripes lady, I'm not even out of my belt."

"Lady nothing, the key-pad…try the key-pad…like a count-down."

We scrambled back upright then nudged and nudged the squares around to shuffle the hoped for results. "Nothing!"

Disappointed, we sat back down on the top corner hearthstone again and looked at each other before bursting out in laughter.

Our hands were blacked, our faces, too. "If Daddy Red or my brothers saw me now, they'd see your hand prints all over my blouse and britches; then too, I'm covered with soot from the heels of my boots up to the top, back side of my knit logger's cap. As for you, only your palms, elbows and knees are sooty."

I cupped her giddy face in my trembling hands, "Maggie, I'm in love with you and want to marry you, too…Leap year or not."

"Yes," changed to more whispered, "Yes, yes, yeses."

Just as we stood up to go back to Annie's home 'n saying, "We gotta' clean up and get on down to the party before all hell and hound dogs are sent after us."

Leaning my hand against the entire matrix, in order to stand up and help Maggie to her feet also, the panel pushed into its frame a couple inches. We both heard a click, like a breach-loader. We turned toward the sound just as the top stones began to pivot away.

With the renewed full moon's light, we peered inside to both see an old fashioned, stagecoach strongbox.

There was barely room for my hands to lift the box out. I cussed then apologized as I tried to reach in but skinned my knuckles.

"Maggie, you try. If Lorena Anna put these in here, her hands were probably smaller than my paws."

"Gently, carefully," she pleaded with herself, even trembling with anxiety then the strongbox was free and lifted up on the edge of the hearth.

It didn't seem to be made with a lock. Its decorations looked like an oriental puzzle. Sliding checkered squares around again like we had for the first key, and pressing it inward, the one-third square meter lid opened smoothly.

Maggie almost cried as she whistled, "...perhaps it's the manuscripts?"

Their edges seemed partly charred and brittle; they were certainly aged. The top page looked like a wanted poster, "Wanted,...Dead or Alive,...Alias Tex Buda, 1876,...Reward, ...$40,000,00!

The etched print looked up at us as if he was smiling a timeless secret.

I jerked off my duster, re-closed the lid and gingerly wrapped the treasure into a secure packet.

This time, when we stood up, we froze, as another loud click seemed to echo off the nearby mountain's faces. The wrought iron damper chain began to click away around each sprocket's tooth and the ground grumbled beneath our feet.

Although tenderly bearing the bundle in both our arms like a new child, we jumped away. With our heads looking back over our shoulders, we almost fell trying to flee some imagined booby trap.

Trap was the right word, part of it at least. A trap door began to fall away right under the edges of our feet. At least we had jumped out of the way for its collapse. Right there before us was a black hole into which a veritable waterfall poured into nothingness. In fact it sounded like the roar, which a dragon might make. I picked up a charred block of stone and dropped it down the opening. It bounced back and forth like ricochets a long time before it rattled away into the flush of a huge maw.

Breathing a sigh of relief, we could see a short span of attached iron ladder, which ended about twelve feet down next to a side opening of the pit. I asked, "Was it some sort of chamber?"

"Or possibly," Maggie suggested, "It goes into the mountainside; do you think it's an escape tunnel?"

"I sure don't know, but I don't want to just leave it open. Let's try something."

Re-opening the strong box, Maggie removed the stack of wire-bound papers. I shut the lid and replaced the strong box in its original receptacle.

The trap doors didn't budge. Remembering Lost Ark movies, I checked around for a rock of approximately equal weight as the manuscripts, placed it in the strong box and knelt upright beside Maggie's legs. This time, the damper chain wound backwards and the trap door lids re-closed.

Both of us simply stared wide-eyed and speechless at each other. Still trembling from fright, she kept the bundled "baby" in her arms as we scattered bits of trash over the area for concealment, then we hurried away to Annie's.

"Maggie, may we be married on Easter Afternoon?"

With one more kiss and skipping steps, she answered, "Yes."

Beyond their sight and hearing, a large shadowy shape stumbled back into the tree line and let go with a low rumbled growl, sort of a snarl, before disappearing into further shadows. The shape was like a large man that trekked straight back down the mountainside's several switch back turns of Annie's new driveway.

* * *

Brave Combo's polka music rattled the rafters as many couples swirled around the Leavenworth Community Center's wood flooring like drumbeats.

In back near the punch bowl and refreshment table, Daddy Red looked down on his wristwatch and fretted to his youngest son, "They shoulda been here by now."

Tiny, Maggie's next older brother, said with a big grin, "Pops, you saw as clear as we all did. That fellow made her heart into a sugar glazed donut."

"It's late. I don't like her not letting me know what's going on. I couldn't'a stood another daughter as unruly as she is. God blessed her mamma when He took her the day Maggie was born."

"You know as well as I do what's going on. We'll be lucky if their sparkin' don't set off a forest fire. They'll be here, eventually. I'm more concerned about where Bristol is; he's never missed being any-wherever she's at."

"Well, he's crazy to show up any-wherever's near me after that bastard put his slap on her face."

"Pops, crazy has no fear. She gave him a broken nose for that mouse already."

"Yeah, that wildcat of ours flung his ash tray exactly where she thought he wasn't expecting it; heavy glass ashtray, too. Shoulda' gouged out his eyes as well as doubling him over with a kick in his gonads."

"Get your brothers. Were going to have a talk with Mr. Buddy Red and Black Boots. I can tend to Bristol later…well, me and nine friends in this magazine clip!"

CHAPTER SIX

Half an hour later, the Cole clan, Tiny, Tad, Ted, Tim, Tom and Daddy Red, sat inside their 4 x 4 gawking at Annie's new driveway. Tom, tucked in the pickup's bed, noticed what made matters worse than a nick on a sharper edge. "Damn it! There goes Bristol's cab; he's got no lights on either. He's up to no good, but good riddance. See, he was parked up behind that grove of trees."

Ted added, "He's made a turn around so as to head back downhill in a hurry if he needed it to be so."

"I'll deal with him later." In the pale light of the last half of the moon's eclipse, Daddy Red then ordered, "Take the driveway, son."

Hardly three turns along several switchbacks up to the hanging valley, Tad admired, "Hell, Pops, do you think Morgan did all this by hisself?"

"Well, son, I'll ask him that before I skin his ass and give the rest to you for tanning."

Tom jumped forward as they hit one rump-bumpity-do that cracked his head against the cab's back window. "Ouch, there's no need to go off half-cocked, we'll do that and you do the tanning."

Daddy Red piped in again, "Maybe so, but it will take two maybe three of you to hold Maggie back while I'm in the midst of my patriarchal chores."

They drove too fast for the last curve into the top of the meadow and gouged out some of Annie's orchard. Tim cautioned, "Slow down Tiny, that's all we need to do is get Annie mad at us, too."

Following slowly down the curve up to the circle in Annie's front yard, there were Buddy's and Maggie's pickups. Just then they were lit up in the headlights. Tiny and Daddy Red bailed out with Tim; Tom and Tad before Ted fell out behind 'em. Tiny taunted, "Oh look, Maggie's loaded with some kind of package like a baby."

Ted mimicked Tinys' tone, "A new pair of love-birdies come strolling out of the back forty."

"Sure enough, I don't need to see more," Daddy Red scowled with a deep rumbling Basso voice, "Those sooty marks on Maggie's clothes and Buddy's knees and hands, tell me all the story I didn't want to hear."

Tad warned, "Oh, their tracks is all over each other's sure to shorten even Daddy Red's fuse."

Maggie'd overheard enough, stopped short, dead-heeled in the other direction and said, "Oh, shit! Buddy, run! I'll hold 'em off."

"What? Like hell, give me a little credit."

"Buddy, you don't understand. I said, Run!"

Daddy, Tiny and three older brothers were hot-footin' in a bee-line to separate Buddy from Maggie.

Out of the dark, off the upper porch, came the sweetest little voice to accompany a couple loud hammer clicks, "Stop right there you noisy sons of my bitch sister! Well la-di-da, now that everyone's woke me up for this congregational meeting, y'all better bow your heads for an opening prayer."

"This ain't Bess, its her twin brother Greenlee and both ten gauge barrels will probably cover the entire spread of your sorry batch of buttocks before you can grab hold of your crotchety dispositions."

None of Maggie's family dared move. "And, I saw you tear out three of my apple trees, yonder, so you can turn around with spades in your hands for re-planting…while you're doing that, you can consider the foolishness of your ways."

Annie swung her double-barreled aim slightly and both tires on the side of their rig disintegrated with a *Ker-Pow!*

As those double blasts and flats echoed around the valley, Daddy Red half raged but knew better as they all realized it would be a long and cold walk home.

Annie had already re-loaded, and was sure to have more double-00s in her nightgown pocket. She stated, "From the matriarchal authority vested in me, I pronounce this man, Buddy Morgan, and woman, Maggie Cole, to be husband and wife."

Daddy Red braved, "You're crazier than Rose."

Annie fired double barrel words right between his further step toward Buddy, "No, I'm a crazier mother-bitch than Rose."

Daddy Red froze, looked down just a bit, shifted his feet, filled up a deep breath with frustration, cocked one elbow up with his hand on a hip and complained, "You didn't ask if anyone's something to say against these two 'up-to-no-goods-but-hell-fire!'"

Annie nodded the double barrel Greenlee in agreement. "So, thank you for your opinion, Amen. Now you either get to fixing my apple trees; start walking home, or settle down up here on the porch so we can figure who and when we're having the Christian Church or charity of your choice and State authorities certify this union."

She didn't wait for any more of their answers. "The only reason you're blustered is because Maggie won't be your nurse and housemaid anymore. Ta-ti-ta-ta-ta! You'll have to make do for yourselves. It's about time these five big brothers went out and married up; maybe you too, except I doubt that many women are to be found in this entire state who's crazier than me."

Without stopping she declared, "Make up your minds. Say it now, or damn your hides and you'll be holier than thou art in these remaining and immediate seconds of your bitter old lives; eight, seven, six, five, four…three…"

Daddy Red turned pale, "Peace! Annie, Peace! From all of us, you win."

Maggie hadn't moved till then, squealed for joy and ran crying the last few yards into her Daddy's arms.

Now bearing the secreted and treasured manuscripts, Buddy took the handshake of each five brothers before handing the bundle back to Maggie.

Daddy Cole didn't speak a word as they faced off to each other. Buddy said, "It'll take me a little while to make our set of rings. In the mean time, I'm going to be almighty busy re-building a house back yonder, so Maggie and me can stay proper sheltered to honor her and the rest of y'all."

As he and Buddy climbed the stairs with Maggie jumping three stairs at a time to hug Annie, Daddy Red remained silent, considered, then asked, "If we can help, will you ask us first?"

"Yes, sir, that's a given word next to the promise I made Maggie less than an hour ago."

Before we sat down together, once more, I shook Daddy Red's hand, but his bear-hug was not one I'd like to enjoy twice.

Grandma Annie kept her Greenlee across her rocker's armrests. What Daddy Red said next, sent a chill up the spines of Maggie, Annie, and me. "Bristol's rig was parked under cover on the road. He took off down the mountain after we showed up."

I simmered with having a problem which I'd rather take care of now. Considering a half moment, I said as a matter of fact. "Your brothers will ride back down with me, then Daddy Red and y'all can take care of particulars. Stay here though. Daddy Red can drive your truck home. I'll be back before breakfast."

"Oh no you don't!" Maggie's concern was plainly voiced.

Buddy's look was icy cold from his pale blue eyes. He answered with a smile, "Maggie, your brothers and I are just going out for a bachelor party."

Annie reached up her hand and fixed on Maggie's wrist, "Do go and wash up your face and hands; your extra clothes are still in my closet!"

Maggie was clearly upset but suggested as she turned to do as Annie told, "Our wedding will be on Easter afternoon, March 23rd of next month."

Without words heard, the Cole brothers piled in or onto Buddy's truck and disappeared beyond the tree line.

Daddy Red didn't disagree. In fact he was already smiling

while considering what he'd need for a wedding feast. He'd already flicked over a couple 3 x 5 pocket notebook pages.

When Maggie returned in a black sheath dress, she was still carrying the mystery bundle on her lap. She set it atop a small table between herself and Annie.

Recognizing Tiex's wanted poster, Annie leaned forward, hands to her mouth and gasped. "Lordy, lord child, that's Annapurna's unpublished manuscripts!"

The double barrel Greenlee hit the porch and discharged. The bundle of papers exploded into a pulverized cloud of tatters and dust.

CHAPTER SEVEN

Down the mountain, about a quarter hour later, Tiny suggested, "We should maybe look for Bristol at the 'Devil's Postpile.' Its an all-night strippers' place in Leavenworth."

Buddy excused Tinys' suggestion, "Show me where he lives first."

East of Highway 2 at Cole's Corner, across the tracks, stretched a row of homes, tenements and trailer parks. Tiny pointed, "Beyond that last curve, his cabin's around the back of the ridge."

I pulled up easy and backed for heading away, "Tiny, I'll be right back. I'm trusting you to stay quiet for me to do the job I'm best at getting done alone."

Tiny's brothers kept quiet as I shucked my firearms, some wire and a few gimmicks. Skirting the trees, I crept near enough to the porch to understand Bristol kept a loose dog; I also saw his truck was not here.

As soon as I drew off a couple feet of duct-tape, his canine reacted to the noise. As it charged around the corner of the house, just like that, I had his snout taped shut to a front paw, which left a very upset three-legged, wide-eyed mute tethered to a back yard stump.

Off his front porch, a springy sapling sprouted through rotted planks. I lashed a length of broken stool to one end. On second thought, I saw a bucket of rusty bolts so I tethered it as well. Checking to see if the load was not too much, I secured the other end of the wire to the tip of the bent bough.

When he'd come home, the hoped for result would show all over his face for a while.

That was my first booby trap. Freeing the two front planks of his porch, where he'd likely step, I turned their nails to point up.

The third rigging was a note on his front door; an invitation of sorts to his choosing. "Sorry we missed you. We didn't want to forget inviting you to our March 23rd wedding."

I added a P.S. as an afterthought. "I'll be waiting where you can't see me, until I tap you on the shoulder."

My final, last trigger would dump a sack load of gathered dog scat onto his head.

Would they all work? It was anybody's guess.

The band of brothers were still quiet but nervous as I appeared by the drivers' side door.

At one time, I heard five, "Jeeza Craps!"

Climbing in to leave the way we came, Tiny exclaimed, "Damn, I liked'ta pissed my pants. Where'd you come from…outta thin air?"

"Show me how to get to the topless bar you were speaking of."

Our next stop was Leavenworth and Tiny's brothers were shivering from exposure.

Good luck follows fate. Bristol's truck-cab was on the downhill slope of the parking lot. Within ten more minutes, I'd rigged the brake released as soon as he'd open his door, stole his license plates and tail light bulbs and poured lube oil along his wipers.

"OK, let's have a look-see at these babes, kinda' like we was havin' a bachelor party."

As late as it was, still over twenty rigs were parked around the old barn turned into an XXX 24-hour club. Four bouncers manned the front door; each one about the size of trees and scarred faces or broken noses to match the looks of their bark.

To Tiny and his brothers, I sized up about like a half-pint. They were well acquainted with the proprietors and bouncers.

Tiny proudly introduced, "Maggie's fiancé!"

Surprised expressions filtered through their passage between broad shoulders and now or then a motorcycle mamma that looked like two roller derby queens after going through the junk-yard's compactor. Then I recognized her, "Gretchen Will?"

She left her old man's side and grabbed onto me! Looking around behind, she declared, "Damn, kiddo, you still got any ass end at all?"

Offering her as much smile as I dared in front of Dave Will, I answered, "Hey, Boo, what it is was left over after leaving a gal named Katrina in Na'leans."

Gretchen blinked and said, 'You, too? Dave and me set on our roof nearly four days without water."

I hugged her back as much as I could. "Tiny, Tad, Ted, Tim, Tom, these are good friends, Dave and Gretchen Will.

Dave, an old Harley friend and older Viet Nam Vet, began to shake hands and share congratulations after I added, "They're to be my new Brothers-in-law this Easter afternoon."

Gretchen almost cried enough tears to fill a shot glass and called out, "Drinks on me, wheee! Are we going to have a ball tonight!?"

The crowd bellied up towards the bar. There he was; at the back faro table, tipped back on a chair 'bout to come undone if he so much as wiggled. The half empty bottle dolloped his shot-glass again. Already sulking, the expression on his face was pure poison. The scab across his broken nose didn't look like any good came of it.

Liking the crowded group of back-slapping buddies, I edged toward Bristol's table with my face sorta' turned toward the crowd. The Cole brothers went silent, others, too. Gretchen's laughter easily was the only other sound heard above the din.

One more side step backwards and I let myself trip. My butt hit the edge of his round table. It flipped up a solid whack cutting a gash under Bristol's chin. His bottle toppled end over end spraying whiskey sloshes in little mid-air spirals.

Already flopped far back in his chair, he cracked the back of his head on the wall. His chair's legs went down beneath his ass end. He screamed from a likely broken tailbone, then erupted out of the corner at me, table flying, chair disintegrating and shot glass finally crashing into shards across the floor.

By then, everything I saw was in slow motion. Neat as can be, I latched onto the neck of Bristols' flying bottle and backhanded a swing that caught him mid-stride on his already bothersome nose and mouth. He sort of teetered like a tree after timber was called out and I sort of flipped up a sharp boot into his balls and tender broken tailbone.

He burped out half a dozen broken teeth and kept coming like a bull. There was a clear shot up and around a connection of his jaw, ear and neck. I gave it all my weight through my fist. His body twisted to catch up to his brain and he spiraled down onto the floor.

I reached down and began dragging his 350 pounds out to the bouncers. "Sorry guys," I apologized, "I tripped and fell against his table. Could y'all help him to his truck?"

Turning around to get back between some friendly shoulders, some stood with drinks half raised and mouths as opened as their eyes for what just unbelievably occurred.

Gretchen broke the trance and shouted "Hallelujah," grabbed hold of me and kept silent about the trembles that gripped my entire body."

Outside, we all heard a bloodthirsty, bone-broken, scream.

The bouncers broke out laughing after looking outside the door in the early morning rain. "Bristol just had a little trouble with his parking brakes; his foot got run over by his front tire."

For the next hour, we hooted and hollered for more as the entire girl's line-up tried to shag all the loggers after stripping down to hard-hats and lace-up boots.

Just before daybreak, flanked in the middle of the Cole Brothers Brigade, I staggered out to the Green Dragon. "Tom's the designated driver," Tiny exclaimed as they heaved me into the trucks' bed, with a tire iron for a pillow.

On the way home, not far from Bristol's dump, we passed a small squadron of Highway Patrol vehicles. Bristol was raging in the brightness of all their flashing lights, while six officers were cuffing him for transport. Bristol's rig was headed back in the direction we just left behind. A large tow truck already had his unit hooked up for impound.

I might be lucky if I didn't see him again until after Maggie and me had our honeymoon. Then again, I might be luckier if I survived Maggie's temper before sunrise.

Well enough, Tom got us back to Annie's before dawn broke, without taking down anymore of Annie's orchard. Horn blaring, tires spitting dirt like a mud buggy, they spun a hooker on the picket fence, and rolled me out inside the gate.

Daddy Red woke up, jumped off the porch, ran along the side of the fleeing pickup and was hoisted over the side panels by Tad and Ted.

They tore away in my mud slinging green dragon before Annie could fire off another double-barreled volley as a fond farewell until we meet again.

I tried to sit up, but Maggie staggered down the stairs with another bottle of Annie's berry brandy. Slurring a bit she raised my head by the roots of my hair and said, "Woo…whoa, I hope…hic…you didn't…think…hic…you could have…burp…all the fun."

Annie descended the stairs with her own reserve on equilibrium. "Children! Go to bed…before you catch your death of cold."

Braced against each other, Maggie and me slowly brought ourselves upright, only because we were leaning in each other's arms. "Hey, I like you. Can I take you home?"

Side by side, we threaded ourselves into the basement

where Maggie and Annie'd made up the guest room into a honeymoon suite.

Annie smiled, tipped up her already empty tin cup and muttered, "Oh, God forgive me, but if I don't die tonight, let me suffer a few more days till after the wedding, Amen."

CHAPTER EIGHT

A hangover wasn't anything new. As a Jack Mormon, I expected it. What I didn't expect was Grandma Annie wielding my digital camera. Blinding flashes kept exploding inside my consciousness. I blinked hard twice before I could lift one eyelid. My skewed views in any direction were all wrong. I must have passed out on my knees and neck and both shoulders with my nose buried in the wrinkles of a bed sheet.

My back hurt. I groaned, blinked my one open eye again and managed to lift the other eyelid halfway. I felt groggy like a heavy, soggy, warm blanket was piled over my back.

Annie flashed a few more pictures and my soggy blanket groaned first then screamed, right in my upturned ear. I was shoved hard over sideways and finally, wide-eyed, looked up at Maggie.

Annie was laughing so hard I thought she'd die. Apparently looking at the slide show of photos, she began laughing all over.

Maggie put her hands across her bare shoulders as I turned to look at her undressed beauty.

"What, what? No! Give me those…Annie, no…"

Annie toddled off upstairs, turned and whispered loudly enough, "Hurry, change into these and clean up; we have to get some size measurements for your wedding dress," then locked the door.

I seemed to be rusted in a half drawn up position,

although tilted over on one side. My Carhartts were tugged down to my thighs. My one boot was pulled off but the other was still on my left foot. My shirt was all shoved up to my chest and neck with one arm not all the way out of a sleeve. I must have snored a lot of Homer slurp because my cheek and beard was still damp and smelled like stale cigars.

Well, Maggie, speechless as she was sputtering expletives, was more beautiful, from a man's biased perspective, and very, what's the word, tousled. Her blond hair was wild.

She wasn't dressed in her usual clothing habit; sometime last night, she'd tried to dress in a slinky, black sheath fit for a night out on New York. Apparently, she couldn't get her one arm through its strap on that side.

My head started to calve off in separate slices before crashing between my ears and teeth. "Oh God," I prayed, "Where's the Iron Worker with his bottle of welder's oxygen?

Maggie was scrambling to re-juggle her one arm and breast into and under the cover of her "Diva Sheath." Next, she checked over her mid-section and crammed both feet into those snug, faded denims. I'd swear they were painted on.

I must have smiled at witnessing a long-held women's secret. She locked her grasp on the waistband and kicked her feet up vertically into the pant legs as her sheath and gravity responded appropriately…all while propped up on the backs of her elbows. As soon as she rocked down into a cross-legged, sitting position, she kicked at me, "Did we do anything last night?"

Her voice almost sounded like she was on the edge of crying. I answered, "I can't remember more than Annie said, "Go to bed!"

As she squirmed out of the sheath and into her blouse, Maggie corrected, "No!" she said, "Children, go to bed!"

Well, looking down to find my belt was buckled up and my zipper was not down, I answered, "I guess not…seems like we both passed out in awkward, if not compromising positions. Was I imagining or did Annie have a camera?

Maggie did cry this time and blurted in tears, "Yes!"

While trading this banter, I straitened my clothes properly, too. I reached for her to hug and she slapped my hands away, groaned again before sinking in my embrace like a little girl, who hoped to heaven that she'd not crossed into big womanhood before her wedding night.

I started to kiss her but we both smelled like too much morning after. Still staggering with her hand to soothe a fierce headache, she grabbed a towel off the dresser table, then shooed me out the front door from inside the bathroom doorway.

Oh, Annie had facilities indoors… those sorts for women's needs. I closed the front door to the ground level porch and staggered toward the little white house.

I looked up to the direction of Annie's voice, "Hurry up, coffee's still hot," but the direction of my gaze was into the blazing light of a fine afternoon sun. Pain streaked into my eyes like needle daggers. Arriving inside the outhouse, I folded into a wretching heap…until cleared of bitters. Annie's herb garden was closest. I grabbed a fistful of oregeno and rosemary, chewed until I could spit and headed for the sauna.

I shouldn't take it for granted. I should remember to thank Annie for everything she does with diligence. My clothes filled with steam, too, as I doused another bucket on the hot rocks. Last night's smoke and stink permeated the sauna's confines.

Deciding, "That's enough," I staggered out, shied away from the defensive geese and realized I'd have to jump through a thin sheet of ice on the stream to rinse out and wash off. I figured, "I'd likely freeze, but here goes."

After baptizing myself, clothes, boots and all, I surfaced and expelled all my breath then sunk to the bottom of the pool until the cold actually made me feel warm. When I came up for air, I sloshed half frozen and completely shrunk of manhood to the back porch.

I felt sure both old and young ladies were on the front porch, so I stripped butt naked by the back window, bolted upstairs to dry off vigorously and redressed. After pulling on my gaucho boots, I stuffed paper towels into my Noconas.

I sauntered back downstairs to go out the front door and join Maggie and Annie for much needed coffee. Whistling, thinking I was the only one at home, I was mistaken, badly mistaken. Annie must have had half the Mormon's Relief Society and Leavenworth Quilter's Club in her living room.

They were already tending to wedding preparations as I stopped in total shock at the realization of my strip and streaking show only moments ago.

Several women lowered their bifocals and continued itty-bitty stitches in a multi-colored quilt designs while others worked pattern pieces of sparkling white satin onto a dressmaker's mannequin.

I'm sure I blushed but before the front door closed, I heard giggles change to guffaws, and then to gossip. Face it, I told myself. This is a once in a lifetime bad experience.

Maggie and Annie were each wearing sunglasses. Annie was alone on the two-seater's, swinging chair. Maggie had a simple yellow and blue dress on with tape measure still draped around her neck. I smiled and let her have a kiss on my cheek.

Annie patted beside her so I sat down there. It was too quiet. I looked from one darling to the other, "What's up?"

"Tell us what happened to you last night," was spoken too simultaneously and too quickly.

I thought, "…my discernment may still be a bit foggy; but I sense a suspicious cover-up."

I repeated slower, "What's up?"

Neither responded at first, then Annie said, "My friend, Jimmie Lou, Dr. Nobles' wife, said he was on duty at the emergency room last night."

I began to get a picture of Bristol being escorted by the police into the ER for the good doctor's look-see.

Both loves of my present life, especially Maggie, smiled the sweetest smile of reconciliation as Annie continued Mrs. Nobles' gossip. "It appeared Bristol walked into a door with nails poked through it. Actually, Jimmie Lou said, 'His face looked like someone going through two doors.' He'll have difficulty sitting down, shaving, or eating for a while. His jaw is broken, he's lost several teeth, his nose is re-broken, and he has a cracked tailbone. The back of his head and his chin took twelve stitches to close both gashes…and his left foot was run over by the front tire of his truck."

"Is that all?"

"Well, yes, if you discount the report that he smelled like a heap of dog manure and was nearly scalped by a bucket of bolts...or that's what Bristol reported to the police."

Maggie added, "He's filed charges against you for animal cruelty. You'll have to give your story to the police."

Yeah, well, I was duct-taping an invitation on his door to attend our wedding, when his dog attacked me.

Annie and Maggie nodded their heads with those pursed lip smiles and hand gestures for; "Good, and OK," but still remained too silent, too closed.

I looked around for some other clue, some other something...the table was gone...there was an odd cluster of holes in the wall, which had been freshly painted with whitewash..."Where are the manuscripts?"

Again, neither, Annie or Maggie offered so much as, perhaps, "...oh, they're in a safe place?"

Then, Annie volunteered responsibility, "I did it."

"What, 'did it', are we referring to?"

Maggie spoke softly. "We had an accident, nearly a very bad, serious accident."

Annie put additional information to Maggie's revelation, "Mr. Greenlee fell off my lap and discharged...almost taking Maggie's head off..."

"So, where are the manuscripts?"

"Gone!" from Maggie's mouth was followed by, "Dust! Tatters!" from Annie's word.

"Oh...oh."

After a hesitated moment, I added, "So you drank Annie's Berry Brandy?"

"Uh-huh."

"Is there anymore left?"

"Na-huh. Drank it all."

"All of it!" I considered remembering how much I'd consumed. Each of us stared blankly, speechlessly at each other.

In silence we sort of focused on Little Annapurna's crown of snow. It gleamed like a wedding tiara. Her mountainous, windblown face remained under a golden, pink veil of late afternoon before sundown. A pair of distant eagles performed a courtship ballet. Periodically, marmots could be seen scurrying for shelter amid jumbled scree slopes after emitting their shrill whistled warnings. This evening was going to be spectacular.

One by one, Annie's friends filed out to bid adieu until tomorrow's work assignment. Several congratulated me for the new driveway.

Dr. Nobles' wife even kissed my cheek. "Thank you for what you did. Maggie never deserved a louse like Bristol. But, you watch your back. He's sworn to kill you when he gets out of jail in three months." She hugged and kissed me again, "I wish you were my son."

As the last of the women got into their vehicles to drive away, we heard more, muffled laughter. Maggie stared, "Are you blushing?"

Annie added, "What happened in there?"

"In where?"

"The house, before you came out?"

"Hmmm, nothing you won't hear through more gossip."

I saw my camera on Maggie's lap and made the effort to not only divert Annie's curiosity, but also get Maggie to look in a different direction. "Look! Fawns."

In the instant, I had my camera and punched up the photo file. Our shocking review brought up my deep and long laughter to tears.

Maggie blushed now and Annie, well, I had to admit, she had an eye for photographic composition. These pictures would delight any blackmail artist's fancy.

"So, Buddy," Annie piped in, "We've got enough light of day left for you and Maggie to show me your discovery."

Maggie stood up with Annie and snatched back my camera and hit delete buttons before I could react with a laugh of glee and relief.

Annie, too, shared a musical laugh for release from a burden, which only pictures in our mind's eye should relegate to one's later memories.

Just as it dawned on me that Daddy Red's SUV was gone and the "Green Dragon" was returned, Annie admitted, "I'll just ride along with you both."

Maggie suggested, "Our next road engineering will need to be an extension to the grist mll and ruins."

In agreement, with Maggie straddling the floor shift knob and Annie buckled to her right side, I added, "I'll have to be more ecology-minded in the basin. It will be a good project for your Pop and brothers to get involved with."

While I tried to drive a passable approach to the grist

mill and ruins, Maggie said to Annie, "We've got about a couple hours before dark."

I parked nearest to remains of the chimney's stack. We got out and I unlocked my toolbox for a lantern and flashlight. Maggie had escorted Annie to the hearth with our warning of the trap door to be avoided.

As Annie sat on the cleared edge, Maggie began shuffling the puzzle tiles. She couldn't remember the number symbols until I joined them. The puzzle box opened with the same gritty sound of grime. Making sure we were all clear of the trap door, I removed the box.

To Annie's surprise, the booby-trapdoor opened with the accompanying noise of its little waterfall. "It sounds like the roar of my old pull-chain toilet, only louder."

I didn't like it. Something was biting on the edges of my consciousness. I turned to scan the outline of trees and hillsides. I had a feeling of being watched, if not aimed at from under distant cover. I didn't say it, but I smelled something like, sour.

Annie maybe felt something, too. I went back to the truck and un-shucked my pistol and rifle, gave one to Annie and suggested, "Move behind the backside of the chimney."

Annie didn't hesitate. Only Maggie asked while turning this way or that, "What is it? Do you think someone is watching us?"

"Child, get around here with me."

Maggie obeyed.

I kept my .28-caliber automatic and carefully descended the rungs of the iron ladder with the lantern looped over my arm. At the ledge, I called up, "See if you can find a stick, …no, the broom in my truck."

Maggie hurried to her chore and wondered out loud, "Are you planning to sweep it clean first?"

Over the dragon's din from the hollow throat filled with the waterfall, I answered, "Yeah. I've never seen so many spider webs. There's a door with iron bars blocking the entrance to the passage."

Turning to Annie, Maggie asked, "I'm going down."

"Alone! Why child?"

Puzzled at more question than beginning a complaint to stop me, Maggie turned with a serious look, "Because…that ladder could be dangerous."

Annie didn't let Maggie finish, "You should have asked me. I'll take the stairs."

To Maggie's astonishment, just like that, Annie flipped another release behind the fireplace, where we were sheltered. A door way opened to a broad stairwell. At the bottom of the stairs, she flipped a light switch. Maggie saw me through the bars on this door with a look of total surprise. Annie unlocked, opened and invited me in.

"Youngsters, tsk, tsk, tsk, …never think to ask old folks for the answers."

I couldn't be more bum-fuddled, "Lights, Annie?"

"Sure, there's electricity in the house, plumbing too, but I've no need to use it. Look around; this is where my still is located."

Maggie began wandering along narrow shelves of wine racks. She wiped years of dust from several prize vintage bottles of wine or champagne.

"Revenuers tried to locate our moonshine works all through Prohibition Years."

I just had to laugh, hugged and kissed Annie's forehead then pulled Maggie close with her laughing as well.

"Grandma Rose told me you might know the secret of Tiex Buda's palace. I apologize for not asking you first."

"Apology accepted, Buddy. Just what did you think was hidden here?"

History, but did you remember something about, 'Dragon's Eyes'"?

"Those are the jewels that he recovered in the ice pools of the Cave of Dragons. Each one is said to be about the size of hen's eggs."

Maggie wondered, "But you were surprised when we brought the lost manuscripts."

"I didn't know about the other puzzle on the fireplace or the outside trap door. This water flow was part of the plumbing's sewer system for the palace as well as my home. It was totally unheard of for pioneer homes and engineers."

I asked, "How extensive are these underground chambers?"

Annie admitted, "I don't know. I haven't been down here since Sam and Tex left and never came back. It was Sam and his brother that ran the still and business of distribution. I made my own wines at the house. I only celebrate on special occasions, like your first date with Maggie and last night's sorrow over destroying our family's history."

Annie picked out a bottle and we climbed out to close all the hatches. Then we saw the footprints: a Bigfoot's prints.

CHAPTER NINE

"Bigfoot!"

"It's just a legend, Maggie."

I believe Annie stated it the correct way for Maggie's sake; as for my opinion, I felt we were being watched or worse. I asked, "Annie, isn't there a creature called a 'Dremo' in Tiex Buda's legends?"

"Yes, even according to Himalayan people of today, they refer to the, 'Bear-Man' or 'Yeti.' Whatever else they do to pass each day or night, they're often blamed for kidnapping young girls. If a pretty young maid comes up missing, I think it's strange that nobody ever blames it on lonely old men. What and whomever, no missing person's bodies come up as forensic specimens."

Maggie added, "How does this Dremo fit into Tiex Buda's life?"

Annie wistfully stared into the past, "I think it's the most beautiful romance story I've ever heard. But we can talk about it after dinner if you can be patient. We still need more detailed plans for your wedding next month."

I mused, "Easter will be a fine deadline for our new home and driveway's reconstruction plans. And the devil's in the details."

"Speaking of the devil, honey," between a hug and a shove, "Have you given any thought to who will be your best man'?

Yes indeed, I'll call my friend and without a doubt, he'll

be here for the wedding day.

Annie wondered, "One of Maggie's brother's?"

"No."

"Your friend from New Orleans, I forgot his name, ..."

"David Will, that's not a bad suggestion but, no. I will keep David in mind if my best friend can't make it, but I have no doubt he'll get here fine."

Annie suggested, "I think Maggie would like to know who it is that she traditionally may be kissed by once or with whom she will dance. What's his name and connection to you."

"You're right. His name is Singer. We were stationed on the same Sniper team in Uzbek until I froze off some toes. He was also our best tracker." Producing the resource nugget for our set of wedding rings, I added, "I met him by chance during my journey here from Elko, Nevada.

"I was changing a blow-out in the middle of nowhere and next thing I know, he's standing there hitching a ride to Wenatchee. He told me he's descended from northern Nevada's Goshutes, or 'Digger Indians,' and I chanced on driving through his back yard."

Annie questioned, "Does he have a last name?"

"No, just Singer, but oh, can he sing!"

Maggie still worried, "Well, I hope he gets here in time to be fitted in his tuxedo."

Annie suggested, "Well fix up some sandwiches while you give him a call."

I'd all but forgotten I had a cellphone. I surely hadn't remembered to keep it charged. Seated on the porch, I opened the slide; I had one notch of power left on the indicator. I punched in Singer's number while hoping I was still in range of service.

My connection went through and Singer's recorder said, "I'm not answering till you leave a message."

I laughed, "Singer, it's Buddy. I'm at my Great Grandma Morgan's home east of Cole's Corner. I'm marrying Maggie Cole this Easter and I'd like you to come up and be my best man. You can ask for directions at The Blue Ox Café, it's owned by Maggie's daddy, Red Cole. Thanks. Bud."

Our tray of Swedish Smorgasbord arrived with Annie's usual flair. Maggie had stripped and dipped into a simple sweater over dress outfit.

She lit a candle and I was reaching before Annie blessed the food, "Heavenly Father, thanks for the hands that saw to this nourishment being here. Please bless it to our use. In the name of Jesus Christ, Amen."

I did blush, apologized and added my Amen after Maggie's.

My steel-drum ring tone sounded: "Hello Singer."

"Caller ID's are great. Is tomorrow too early?"

"Not at all, I'll have some work to do for a few weeks if you're up to it?"

"You knew I'd be there, my friend. Does she have blond hair and blue eyes?"

"You have blue-tooth, I'll send you some pictures of us."

"Does your Great-grandmother live in the Alpine Meadows Wilderness?

"Yes, in fact, we watched Little Annapurna's southeastern face at sundown."

"It's not in my back yard, but I know that region. A lady named Annie sharpened my knives once."

"Just a second." I put the phone on speaker mode. "Do you want to say hello to her?"

"She's a Great Lady, besides a distant ancestor of mine, too."

"What?"

"I'm related to Tiex Buda from his eighth wife."

Annie answered, "I thought he only had seven wives."

"Yes, Annapurna had a mild stroke when she delivered your mamma. They were living with some Mormon friends in the town of Panguitch, in the Territory of Utah. His Bishop told him she needed help around her home and my great great-grandmother married him and moved into their house."

Annie laughed about the news, "We do have a lot to talk to you about, Singer. I can't wait to see you again."

My phone emitted a low-battery warning. "We're going to have a lot more to talk about this; my cell phones about to die."

"See you soon, Bud. Don't let the Bigfoot steal Maggie, Goodbye."

Mildly stunned, I slid the cell phone closed and replaced it in its holster, which I kept looped around my neck."

"I hope I remember where my charger is."

"You two love birds…don't stay up sparking too long; I'm going to bed."

Curling up her legs and resting her head in my lap, I began stroking her face, hair and shoulders. "Do you want a diamond in your rings?"

"With my hands always in dishes or washing loads of diapers, I'd prefer a simple band. Have you thought of a design for our rings?"

I left the diaper loads quietly in my mind. "The pattern of weave is called several things: Mystery braid, Trinity braid, Wizard rings…it's a simple three-in-one plait."

"Is it cast like lost wax or some such method; how will you make it?"

"Sam's old blacksmith shop'll have everything I need. I was thinking of drawing out the nugget into wire…"

Punching me in the shoulder, she pointed a wagging finger, "Don't say barbed wire or I'll cry all over your heart."

"I wouldn't and didn't, or vice-a-versa. It's impossible to mystery braid the gold like my friend does in leather, unless it is done with one wire folded into three strands."

"Oh! May I watch?"

"If I'm not mistaken, proper courtship and traditional weddings consider seeing you in your wedding dress before the ceremony as bad luck."

Smiling with feathered edge kisses with fingertips, "You're the best luck in my life."

"We're people with shadows on the ground."

"What does that mean?"

"Neither of us is perfect, except right now."

"Ooooohh!" Shoving me away, she declared, "This, No, means not yet. I'm going to bed."

"Look at the stars for awhile."

"I've got enough stars sparkling all over inside. Go to bed yourself…upstairs!"

"Well, was it John Wayne said, "Katie, bar the door."
"My name's not Katie, it's Margaret."
"I can see the stars flashing in your eyes."
"Yeah, well I smell a lit stick of TNT in your britches, Goodnight!"
"Goodnight, Margaret, You know I really think I love you more today than yesterday…"
"Good, I've always wanted a spiral staircase in my…our home. I'll love you more tomorrow."

As she shut and locked her door, I turned around the outside of the Green Dragon, unlocked my toolbox and belted on my Beretta 9mm automatic. After checking its clip for a full load, I shucked my 300 Savage from its scabbard and uncapped the scope. Also tucking more ammunition in my vest, I returned to Sam's workshop after a quick sprinkler at the outhouse. I searched around aimlessly before realizing, "I'm out of cigarettes." Then I figured, "…well, I've gone this long without thinking about one…I should quit while I'm ahead."

All through my sparkling conversation with Maggie, I had that same feeling of being watched. I wished Singer were with me right now. I considered going alone for a look around was unwise, but that could wait until Singer would make up the better part of a team.

Lighting a couple kerosene lanterns in Sam's shop, I searched around for a die for pulling wire. It didn't take long and set it up in Sam's old vise. I was hoping to find a box of sheepskins and mallets for pounding out the peach pit into a thin, flat sheet before rolling it into a gold rod to begin pulling out as wire.

ALIAS TEX BUDA

While groaning a bit like a schoolboy with crotch cramps, I located what I needed under dusty back shelves. I knew Annie probably wouldn't appreciate me pounding around, so I set out the things I'd need for daybreak. Besides forgetting about my cellphone, I still fidgeted around my pockets for a cigarette. I hadn't thought about one since running out while building the first roadway entrance up to Annie's home. I could smell little things again, but having a wild night with Maggie's brothers included a cigar. My nicotine receptors were firing with the immediate return to an overload of oxygen.

I felt sure someone was snooping around. Neither Annie, Maggie or me chewed snoose. It was such a small distinction of scent, but there was a drop or two of Bailey's in the smell of this chew.

I returned to my room for the set of BDU's I still kept. Going silently back down to the workshop, I turned off the lanterns and melted into the shadows when incoming clouds blocked the moonlight. I remained along the higher tree line, above the grist mill's bridge and pond. About fifteen minutes later, I saw a shadow moving across the bridge and down toward the ruin's blackened chimney.

Apparently without noticing previous tracks, the stairwell behind the chimney opened and my quarry's shadow hurriedly disappeared below. The glow of the downstairs light bulb outlined the opening. I moved near enough to be ready for who or whatever would leave.

I didn't give him time to shut the stairway. His arms were filled with several stolen bottles. I spoke up as the cold little

9mm circle touched the back of his head. "I'm surprised you didn't drop any of those bottles."

A short, square, bald-headed man's voice answered, "They're too valuable. May I turn around?"

"I've no problem with that as long as you sit down on the edge of the fireplace hearth with them."

Shying away from the portion above the booby-trap's door, he sat still and introduced himself, "Me name's Sean McConnell. I used to be the head of the Revenuer's Team back over eighty years ago."

"So you never could figure out where Sam and Tex had their still. For your information, they're buried in pauper's graves in Buda, Texas. You look and speak like a square-headed Irishman, you love your Bailey's with your snoose."

"I can still box your ears with bare-knuckles if you call me 'Square-Head' again."

I holstered my pistol. He looked to have a good walking cudgel and travelers pouch. His rosy nose and cauliflower ears showed many years of a fighting and drinking Irishman. "No offense meant, but you are trespassing, as well as stealing from Annie's prized, vintage, wine collection."

"Yes sir. Me lips got dry and me eyes bugged out. I couldn't help meself…"

"So, indeed in a slip of better judgment, you did help yourself."

"I'd ask ye this small favor in that its almost St. Patty's Day; let me go and I'll see to it that you have a pot of gold.'"

"Ha-hah! Although, I've been considering, 'You have to be the most diligent Revenuer I've had the chance to meet in my short lifetime…hmmm should I guess, less than about half your lifetime?"

"I'm 99 years old. Widowed last year in Bellingham."

"We're you checking us out earlier?"

"Yes, well…I was more particular to the finer old lady t'was with you two youngsters…until that Bigfoot showed up."

"Let's go to the house. I'm a bit shy of meeting any more strangers. I feel like we're better off together."

"You felt it, too. I'm guessing just above us behind that craggy outcrop."

Hoisting my Savage to point behind my back, I asked, "Sean, take a look-see through my scope."

Only a second later, Sean crossed his Catholic heart and murmured, "Saints preserve us. I just looked into his red eyes and me hair kind of bristled, then he just disappeared."

"Good enough for now. Let's go, Sean. I'd rather have more friends around me now coming so close to getting married on Easter afternoon."

CHAPTER TEN

Annie smiled, "You've all brought back magic to my kitchen table."

It was shortly filled for breakfast. She and Sean pretty much fell in love at first sight. They'd actually met during prohibition years, but Annie had married Sam Morgan. It was Maggie's and my turn to be mildly surprised.

Singer and his family showed up next…out of thin air. He introduced his red-haired, freckle-faced wife, Jan Singer; one son, Joseph Porter Rockwell, 10; and two daughters; Betty, 5, and Ann Singer, 6; each were miniature images of their parents.

Maggie knew immediately who our ring-bearers would be. It seemed no surprise to me that we had a veritable family reunion going on. No sooner than the Singers were introduced, Daddy Red, Tiny, Tad, Ted, Tim and Tom arrived.

After hugs and handshakes rounded out the crowd, Annie invited the children to do some morning chores: "Please, feed my cows, horses, chickens, ducks and geese and bring in the eggs."

Jan helped Maggie keep up with pancakes, bacon and eggs, coffee and toast with fresh-picked, strawberry jam. They may as well have been sisters.

While Sean took care of washing dishes, he told Annie and Singer, "My family came north from the end of the railroad building at Promontory Point, north of the Great Salt Lake, in what was then the Territory of Utah."

Maggie hurried away to retrieve my recorder and set it on Annie's magic table, kissed my forehead then returned to the wood burning heart of the home.

Singer added, "Tiex Buda would also have been there when the Gold and Silver Spikes were set. But, any Chinese, Indians or Blacks were prohibited from attending the ceremonies."

Annie filled in more historical notes, "In fact, those workers were left virtually in the Salt Lake Desert after being told their jobs were finished."

Singer looked down his families' trail,. "Tiex's family, now including my great-great-grandmother, came through the Goshute's backyard till connecting with The Oregon Trail."

Annie told how she'd heard, "Together with several Chinese families, they settled into farming and orchard cultivation along the Eastern Cascades. As a holiday kick for the 1876 Centennial, they built a hot air balloon for a little sightseeing; that's when they found this hanging valley.

"Tiex employed several families in building their Oriental Style Palace. They actually lived in smaller homes at the back of the valley. The last ones fled when Japanese family members were removed during World War II; it didn't seem to make any difference between Chinese or Japanese. They were all Orientals. Some of their homes' foundations remain to this day. I haven't seen them for a couple decades."

After a silent moment of solemn reflection, Sean added to their review, "My kith and kin also worked on building that railroad. They later moved on to the coastal fishing and logging cities of Seattle and Bellingham. We lost more relatives outside Dawson Creek after they followed the Alaska gold rush migrations."

Changing the subject a little bit, Annie backtracked and asked Singer, "I never heard where Tiex's family lived before leaving Utah Territory; can you give us that story?"

Singer started, "Panguitch is in the heart of a long, fertile valley. It's about two weeks south of Salt Lake City by wagons. Political history of The State of Deseret, after an 1848 Treaty of Guadalupe-Hidalgo, began having issues that were constant sources of conflict between the U. S. Government and early Mormons. Bigamy and Polygamy were two of the principle issues, but not all of them. In 1850, the U. S. government made the, Territory of Utah."

Jan let him catch a breath, adding, "Polygamy became a Republican Party issue in 1856. The polygamy issue wasn't resolved until thirty years later, in 1890, when Wilford Woodruff presented a revelation called, the 'Manifesto.'"

Jan continued like an American history professor, "The next big break off of Mormons came from those who didn't agree. They purported, the president and prophet of the church caved in to outside political pressure…just to become the newest state of the Union. Those folks rejected Wilford's leadership and began to break the newest laws of the nation. After they were excommunicated, many polygamists went to isolated geographic locations, Canada, or Mexico. Those communities within the U.S. are still running around as fugitives."

"Moderns named themselves 'Fundamentalists', but they're still fundamentally wrong. They reject the laws of the land, the church's leadership, as well as socially accepted standards of age for adult's rights of choice. Recent efforts by the Utah State Attorney General's office made it too hot for most of the remaining Utah groups so they moved to West Texas. That's sure to backfire because of smoldering hatred from other Christian communities."

Singer backtracked, "But, in the midst of the Civil War, when the U.S. Government outlawed bigamy in 1862, agents came to Panguitch. Those officers had to stay at the Cameron Hotel. Whenever they arrived, priesthood boys went out that night to warn their assigned families, 'Get the other wives and children out of their homes, except the first wife.'

"If the government agents found more than one wife in a home, the husband went to prison for a year, after losing all their lands, property and livestock.

"Things weren't getting any better after The Mountain Meadow Massacre, during previous bad times of, 1857-1858, when war was declared against Mormons in the then, State of Deseret.

"Tiex and Crow, with their families, bid goodbye to Cameron and others who were arrested, then fled north with his families to the Logan railroad boom area until after the golden Spike connected the first trans-continental rail line from East to West coasts in 1869.

"Tiex and Crow offered to help the Chinese labor groups who wanted to go up to the Northwest. They got as far west as Elko and came north through the homeland of Tiex's eighth wife. She died after delivering my great-grandfather and is buried in the Jarbidge Wilderness. To my knowledge,

Crow stayed there and married my mother's sister."

Before we finished our last cups of coffee, Postum or Pero, Annie reasoned, "Of all the past laws that might be considered unconstitutional, plurality of wives is at the top of the list. It violates freedom of religion and today more so than previous years; African, Middle Eastern, or Asian families have been granted citizenship or been welcomed as foreign guests in the country regardless of having more than one wife."

I think we all marveled at having stories and ideas like these to share. Maggie asked Annie, "You were going to tell us the love story of when Tiex met Lorena Annapurna."

"Child, it would likely be sundown before I could finish. We have to get started on fixing up some lunch and dinner for the men while they work on a road up to your place. I'm sorry to disappoint you twice now, but let's get some work done while its daylight. Why these tales are best as bedtime stories anyway."

With that said, the girls took away breakfast dishes. Daddy Red, five brothers, Singer and me began walking out a survey to the farthest reach of the valley. The simplicity of several old Oriental homes offered an additional remodeling opportunity. Nearly sixty years had worked time's magic on their abandoned homes. I don't know who of us was more excited with ideas to also develop this historic community. Sean suggested a Scout Camp or Authors retreat.

Coming back via the palace ruins and the mill, we began a list of materials for restoration work. We began to seriously joke about contacting, "This Old House."

Sean apologized after our first long trek, "I'll be staying closer to Annie and the girls as a go-for-this, or honey-do-that."

By early afternoon, it was storming. Daddy Red invited us down to steak dinner. I had a comprehensive list of needed supplies. "It wouldn't hurt to expedite matters with a backhoe, dozer and grader." I added, "We'll need a fairly large steam-cleaner, too."

It was agreed, "Too much heavy equipment would likely ruin our first access road." We would do better to upgrade it and stabilize any weak spots and run off problems with better gravel and culverts before tackling the new road.

With barely two weeks to complete what we planned, Maggie's brothers could spend time with Singer and me, while she and Daddy Red tended The Blue Ox from 2:00 till 8:00 PM, until two very capable waitresses arrived for Maggie's one job.

We could meet at 6:00 each evening for supper and scheduling the next day's work assignments. Sean and Annie stayed home with the three kids and Jan to help out chores and daybreak meal preparations.

It rained some, snowed a little more, too. Inside the old mill, Singer and I took turns with the steam cleaner. Daddy Red had also brought along a sand blaster. Cleaning the mill house from top to bottom produced an enormous mess. When we finished, we flushed out all the floors. That's what yellow ducks and rain boots are for.

What surprised us most was discovering a late 1890s electrical generator and huge storage batteries. A staircase, not exactly spiral, wound up around the support structure for the windmill drive shaft.

At the top of the loft, a fine view from the East at sunrise would be viewed through Dutch-like, wrap-around windows throughout the day's length till sundown. Its upper deck, or porch was just wide enough for small chairs, table and a rocker. A safety banister could be built with removable planter boxes, urns or vases.

The loft would be our master bedroom. Privacy utilities were easier to remodel from modern supplies: bath, shower, sinks, etc. and toilet.

While Daddy Red supervised roadwork to the grist mill, Singer and I then scrapped out the ruins' old rafter beams to re-finish. Timbers of the palace had collapsed during the past destruction by fire, but they hadn't burned clear through. Perhaps weather at the time had quenched the initial blaze. Time and seasons certainly had weathered away much of the charred surfaces; it certainly added nature's patina on the remaining beam's outside layers. We used some inside the mill.

Tad was the best cherry-picker operator with Tim as a spotter. In half a day, they had the major structural beams and primary laterals stacked and elevated for Singer and me to work over. We bored out old pegs and with Sean's expert eye, had new pegs fashioned for replacements.

Tom and Tiny finished improving the road to Annie's. We might have problems after next winter's storms but for now, we had a strong enough road to bring in heavy loads or equipment. Afterwards, they met us at the millpond to start fencing around the perimeter.

Ted cleared out the millpond, built a rowboat dock and made sure to have a sturdy diving board for the swimming hole. During evenings, upstream, we enjoyed catching a mess of trout with some fly-fishing by suppertime.

Subtly, Singer set up a defensive barrier, as well as a firing range with meter marks in every direction. I enjoyed the shared experience of Joseph's early expert shooting. I also had time to help train the girls to shoot, well at least until Annie came out with "Bess" and Maggie marked a fair ballantine for five hundred yards. Singer had taught his daughters well enough; but we worked on cleaning the weapons as well as firing them.

Maggie and Jan made grocery runs into Leavenworth and met the Relief Society sisters for final fittings on her wedding dress. Her Daddy had hired two more waitresses and a buxom, temporary cook. News of the wedding and construction work for improvements had spread around the immediate countryside from the grocers, barber shops, and beauty salons.

Talking with the Sheriff one morning at the Blue Ox, Maggie learned Bristol had been released and was still surly and mean. She inquired, "If you don't mind me asking a couple questions: 'Is Bristol from Texas, if so, where, exactly…and what is his full name?'"

"He was born and raised in Buda, Texas and served in the Marines Special Forces. The name given on his military records is: Bristol Ochterlony Cobb."

As long as he stayed away from contact with her, Bristol's injuries would eventually heal. His animal cruelty charges were dropped after he'd killed his own dog.

Maggie told me the local news and gossip. I was relieved at not needing any further contact with him. Never the less, I apprised Singer of the situation. Although he enjoyed the story of the booby traps, I now had someone else to be alert for any signs of danger. We had no other experiences with Bigfoot.

As soon as Singer, Tom, Tiny and I had reset the main rafter beams, we also finished framing in the new spiral staircase and set windows and doors.

Sean kept busy running back and forth with the finished cabinet works, chairs and tables from Sam's old shop. He was a master of woodworking skills and Joseph enjoyed his tutoring as well. Sean was also a master electrician. He refurbished the generator's old, worn brushes. He also repacked new straw mixed with heavy grease into all the wooden drive bearings until better quality Babbitt replacements could be forged. With the new paddle wheel working and the windmill blades turning. By the time we'd finished all we could do inside, our new home had wind and water powered electricity.

Annie, with help from Jan's daughters, made flowerbeds and garden plots. The entire valley was bright with wildflowers in bloom. The Honeymooner's home took priority over the ruins.

A pair of newborn calves delighted the kids, which in turn delighted all our memories of their excitement. Three mares dropped foals, too. The Hanging Valley was once more vibrant with life… and death.

Before Annie could bring old Bess to her shoulder one morning, Singer took down my 300 Savage and dropped the black bear that had killed one of the calves. Betty and little Annie took it hardest.

Sean did most of the skinning while teaching Joseph.

They had both bear and calf butchered and curing in the smoke house by that sad nightfall. Tanning would take a little longer and Singer took over with Jan instructing the girls how to properly prepare the hide.

Just five days away from Easter, Maggie pulled me aside and said, "Honey, did you forget we need a marriage license?"

Well, yes I did, blood samples, too. Maggie and Sean informed me, "We'll need a bigger vehicle. Your green dragon isn't big enough to seat all four of us."

To my surprise, Sean had proposed to Annie. We were now going to have a "double-barreled wedding. By the time we got home that afternoon after fittings for tuxedoes, Patriarch Fairbanks and Bishop Sorenson supervised overhauling the ruins with more local volunteers. Dave and Gretchen Will brought a legion of disabled Vets. It was kin to a Barn Raising and GI Party, combined.

On Good Friday, the front half of the ruins had a new truncheon and tile floor for a Texas Style Boot-Scootin' Square Dance. Our secret chambers remained secure, yet also cleaned up until later work could be undertaken.

Sean fixed the stonework on the old kitchen hearth, oven and made the east chimney ready for a Texas style Barbeque. We realized the third chimney had never been attached to the ruins; it was separate. Only after clearing away its debris did we discover it was actually a kiln for firing glazed tiles or pottery.

Daddy Red and Maggie's brothers cleaned out other lower rooms, and mulched them into kitchen and herb gardens.

Singer and Joseph cleared one larger spaced room as a

prepared ring for a Good Friday Gambler's Marble Tournament.

However, Saturday morning was solid gray and wet. Everything was as near to done as everyone could accomplish.

Bad weather didn't break Easter Morning. We prayed and fasted for sunbeams by afternoon.

Without me knowing, Singer had invited old Ranger team members and Dave and Gretchen brought all the available local Veteran's groups. I didn't need my tux after all. The husbands of the Relief Society members made sure I had a set of Formal Dress Class A's.

Sean surprised me even more by presenting me with a brand new custom made Saber, with which to later cut the wedding cake.

Just before sundown, a distant rumbling drew our attention to a possible earthquake. The sound continued to increase until we'd thought a true dragon was going to fly toward us over the ridge top. Just then, a long string of Denton's finest Harley Davidson club members rode single file into the valley.

Tiny surmised, "I better go to town for some more kegs of Olympia Beer."

Following Easter Sunrise services, our weather concern was answered with something better. A double rainbow lit the eastward sky as Singer performed, "The Wedding Song." When he finished, Daddy Red carefully led Margaret's steps down the front stairs with Betty and Ann close behind. To my utter surprise, Annie's bridesmaid was Gretchen and Dave

Will was Sean's best man.

You just gotta know, Gretchen used to be a heavy metal bar bouncer in New Orleans. She's all rings and Tasmanian devil tattoos protecting a heart of love and tears.

Singer was right. His God's name is, 'the Gambler' with another ace up his sleeve to surprise everyone. Dave Will had shipped with one of Sean's last Naval Command Missions.

After walking a rather formal and informal gauntlet of military and motorcycle uniforms, Tiny, Tad, Ted, Tim and Tom stopped with their proud, beaming father as Annie, Margaret, Sean and I stepped into a circle of twelve, small, up-ended, slicum scales.

Following solemn vows, Bishop Sorenson asked the final questions.

After kisses and erupted cheers, a pair of twenty-one gun salutes echoed far and wide. We were showered with fists full of bird seed, more tears, more kisses, dancing, fun and more than enough of Daddy Red's finest food, as well as tube-steaks for all the kids.

Annie and Sean asked Dr. Fairbanks, "Stick around in case we have heart attacks and die on our honeymoon night?

We shared even more laughter and song with more dancing and leftovers…of course remembering to save room for a piece of cut wedding cake.

By sundown, everything had been perfect until Bristol showed up. He was still in the cast on his foot, limped with crutches and had his jaw wired shut. All he offered to sort of hiss out the side of his mouth was, "You did give me an invitation."

Daddy Red came right over and all but tripped on Bristol's foot. Maggie's brothers noticed, too. Although some new girls in the crowd of guests had latched onto most of their attention, they also joined their Pa.

If the new Mrs. McConnell hadn't intervened with a cup of duck soup and a soda pop with a straw for Bristol, she may have seen him being escorted from the property by the seat of his pants.

The Relief Society President stood up and announced, "Let's get this cake cut and open your presents."

The entire Cole clan as well as Denton's HD squad became Bristol's extended shadow for the remainder of the reception.

Both brides' garters were tossed far and wide. If the other women missed the catch, we didn't miss the lady-like hooks and looks latched onto Daddy Red and each brother's strapping arms. Unless I missed my guess, more weddings would be held on these same grounds before Mid-Summer's Night.

By 9:00 PM, the children were fast asleep. Most of the guests had returned home. I wanted to do more for my Squadron and old hometown's motorcycle friends and Dave's veteran buddies…and Singer…and everyone that made this day an eternal memory.

I asked Singer to stay longer; we needed to go hunting as well as explore the underground tunnel systems.

Maggie and Annie's wedding dresses were remarkable. Their gifts and tokens filled Annie's living room. Sean and Annie had new cellphones. We'd sort out the rest later to each other's respective homes.

Jan, Singer and their children took over the upstairs and my loft. There is something magical about carrying sleeping children to their respective beds. The girls had their own double sized, snuggly, German-style *federdeckes* of goose-down underneath which they slept. Joseph had my bunk in which to sleep. Mamma and Daddy had the room with the private upstairs bath.

We gathered on the balcony porch for a peaceful rest and quiet anticipation of Easter Day's meaning and contemplated its beauty. We added new contact numbers in each other's address files. Later, ecstasy waited this long; even longer for Annie and Sean. We could all say in agreement. "May I just sit still as the rest of the world winds back down."

Maggie repeated her new name, "Margaret Ann Cole-Morgan… I love it."

The new Annie Buda Morgan-McConnell reminded her, "We agreed to take these men's names; it's not the other way around. I chose to follow Sean's directions. He's the new head of the family while we remain on this earth. We women are only the neck and with wisdom we can turn their heads in the best direction…mostly."

Sean raised a final toast, "I'll drink to that now, because I chose to hold onto Annie more than the neck of me last bottle."

"Hear, hear!" We all raised our tin cups and carefully sipped.

Maggie spoke first, "I still want to hear Tiex and Lorena's love story."

Annie sat forward after leaning back to rub on Sean's back.

I said, "First, let me get my recorder."

"Why, are you afraid we might not make it through the night?"

Sean smiled, while Maggie laughed, I only added honestly, "Well, yeah! We only have you for this treasured piece of history."

Annie blazed a question out of her ice-blue eyes at me, "Are you making a dig at me for blasting the draft copy into dust?"

I admitted honestly again, "Yeah."

"OK, just checking where we stand."

Sean stood up, headed towards their quarters, I thought he had to use the John but he came right back with a beautiful, leather-bound book. He held it out to Maggie while saying, "Read it together for bedtime stories. Annie and me have to get our beauty rest…if we fit together like spoons and not wake each other from me snoring."

Annie confessed musically again. "We've already finished reading the book for our bedtime stories." Then repeating an earlier injunction she repeated tenderly, while handing us the book, "Children, go to bed!"

Maggie and I were equally astonished. Questions in our minds wouldn't form themselves into words.

Finally from Maggie, "But, I thought the original…well…was blown to bits!"

She opened its front cover with heartfelt reverence. Tiex and Lorena Annapurna's picture were portrayed in an oval frame. Their signatures were beautifully penned beneath their quiet smiles.

ALIAS TEX BUDA

I think both me and Maggie cried real tears of joy as she hugged it to her bosom, grabbed me by the arm and kissed Sean's bald, head and Annie's cheeks. I stood up and shook Sean's strong hand. Annie stood and hugged me too with a kiss. "Children…tsk…tsk…don't forget to ask the old folks for the answers."

Our next stop was to lock our castle door and slowly climb our new spiral staircase…Maggie held the book like a baby. I held Maggie in my arms like a bride.

The muffled sound of the water wheel was as lulling as a rocking chair's loose runner. Like a steady heartbeat, its pulsing rhythm harmonized with our sighs and moaning pleasures.

CHAPTER ELEVEN

Waking up this morning was a far cry from last week's bachelor party hangover. I could smell bacon, eggs, toast and jam. Maggie was all squeaky clean, glowing smiles and sunbeams as she sat sipping some of Jupiter House's finest blend of Balthsazar coffee beans.

The greeting card she handed me was from Amy and Joey, who own the finest coffee shop in Texas.

"Maggie, I have to apologize."

"What for?"

"You deserve a trip for our honeymoon."

"Where are you suggesting?"

"We can make plans for several places, but I want you to see Denton's Arts & Jazz Festival."

"Good enough…when is it happening?"

"April 26th through the 28th. Are you up for a motorcycle ride?"

"I don't know…I've always fantasized about the dangers of riding straddle an 800-pound vibrator. Besides, I'm already saddle-sore from bidding virginity goodbye."

Seeing the volume of Tiex Buda's legends, I noticed a book marker about a third of the way from the beginning. "Tarnation, Maggie, did you stay up all night reading?"

"I wasn't the one who fell asleep. All our good sex simply kept me awake."

"Did you discover any family secrets?"

"Oh, you wouldn't believe…"

"Maggie, I heard a story that Eve told the truth once and look where it got her…but, I'm inclined to trust in everything you'll tell me."

"I could tell you to read it yourself, but I'm not that kind of girl."

Fingering a marked page, she flipped back to the story of Tiex's meeting with Lorena Annapurna and said, "The Cave of Dragons keeps showing up in several tales…it's the place where Tiex's father returns from wars with China before Tiex is born to one of the King's daughters.

"It's also the place your Grandma Rose told about young men going to receive endowments of stones and eyes of dragons, but Tiex goes back after soldiers have killed his father. Tiex's first six wives and children, as well as some of the King of Nepal's family members, are bound together with Small Pox blankets.

"Tiex returned to the sacred place after receiving the commission from this king to deliver retribution and gather together all their stolen treasures to be returned.

"Buddy, I don't understand all that these 'Sons of the Dragons' were taught…they were something like special agents, spies, hit-men and more, all rolled into one. They were taught skills in every ancient form of combat and defense including hypnotism or mind-control."

"Like Jedis?"

"Yes, but not with light-sabers; Tiex, and Krough's names were changed at Ellis Island to Tex and Crow. Afterward, they traveled through the toils of the Civil War while they made clothes and hand-made accessories to sell, like hats and gloves. There was once in which Crow was conscripted and Tiex rescued him with a balloon from the infamous Andersonville. Their adventures during the return trek to be with their new wives in the Jarbidge Mountains before birthing times is another whole story."

Lorena Annapurna saved Tiex's life several times with her own swordsmanship. She even cut off the face of an evil whorehouse Madame who was about to turn him in to the Marshal of a Texas town named Buda."

"Buda, Texas! That's where I found the graves of Annie's husband and his brother."

"Anyway, in the early 1850s of Nepal, Tiex saved a Dremo's child and was being shown a secret vault. The Dremo took his twelve jewels and placed them in a matrix. A vault opened in the wall of the cave. Inside, he found a huge repository of extraordinary biomechanical, dragons and snow leopards."

"Excuse me!"

"Yeah, right…I mean, these things are straight out of dragon legends from the end of the previous world from which Adam and Eve began a new world."

"Are you sure Lorena isn't writing science fiction-fantasy?"

"I don't know. It's all written in first person whenever she quotes Tiex's stories. 'Question remains, 'Where are Tiex's twelve jewels?'"

Before I'd finished two cups and breakfast, Singer called to me with a respectable knock, "Butts, we need to talk."

I didn't wait, kissed Maggie, "I'll be just a minute…" well, only after ungluing another apron lifting embrace, "I'll be right there," while Maggie giggled a mocking whisper, "I'm coming, I'm coming!"

Mostly composed, I opened the door to see Singer dressed in our mountain BDUs, scanning up the ridge to the back of the mill. He turned and pointed for me to look down. Right there at my bare toes were more prints of the Bigfoot.

"It was here sometime last night...circled the place, turned and left up toward that ridge."

Sobered, I looked back at Singer; "It's the same place Sean and I saw someone, or something a couple weeks ago."

"Meet ya' back her in five...?"

"Without a doubt...load for bear." With that said, I went back upstairs at three steps per running pace. I changed into my old set of granite gray and blue BDUs.

Turning to expect Maggie's complaint, she spoke first, "Heard and saw from the balcony. I'll lock up but you two hunters be careful. I'll just read my new book and deal with worrying about my husband being gone for the first time."

Kissing her as she knelt on knees at the edge of our bed, I whispered, "Please call Sean for me. I need y'all to stay alert."

At the top of the stairs, her voice turned me back around, "I love you."

I couldn't go without returning, wrapping her up in my arms and whispered back, "You're the only reason love is now in my world...I love you."

Before I closed the front door, I heard, "Don't miss lunch."

Singer was ready; we both wore BDU's and light systems

from Sniper days. Without speaking, we agreed to backtrack rather than pursue. With only smudges of morning dew, shifted stones and more than a couple of hairs here and there, we found a peculiar slanted cleft near the waterfall. Secluded within heavy cover of old growth trees, an opening appeared hardly more than another separated cleavage of slicum scale.

Singer fingered more hair snagged on bark, another strand on rock above our shoulder's height. This creature could easily stand six and a half feet tall. "Butts, this is not a male...piddle marks under a squat, not in front of standing feet."

"Yeah, Singer, at some time past, this pathway has been well traveled."

We had plenty of room to enter about four feet of an open hallway before a zig-zag into another passage. Sure enough, we were standing inside a den behind the waterfall.

Snapping an IR light stick, our night vision eyes adjusted to the darkness. There was enough ambient light filtered through the cascade to discern everything within the den.

Singer saw them first; narrow gauge mine rails ended at a dump car just inside the falls. From then on, we signed to each other. We moved slowly in tandem from one wall to the other. The waterfall drowned out our footsteps upon loose gravel, for now at least.

"Smell it?" Singer signed.

"Yes," I signed. It had a musky edge to its odor, different from sour and almost like tuna. I expected the wriggling mass of bats above until finding no droppings on the caverns' floor. This cave was odd in that we saw no stalactites or stalagmites, only wet slicum walls of chrome ore with imbedded dikes and seams of other metamorphic rock.

Checking behind us to remember the orientation of the entrance, we proceeded farther into the cavern. I motioned at a junction of openings; to our left, the passage sloped up in the direction of the mountainside, where we suspected our female creature had hidden. If so, we could expect an encounter with her return. To the right, the narrow rails disappeared within darkness. Fading back toward the falls and noise, Singer hunkered in beside a barrier. We kept at opposite sides, yet in sight of each other. My cover was a bit higher on a dry shelf. We chose to keep our pistols holstered in preference to knives.

Not more than seven minutes went by before a shadow moved through the chamber's inner darkness. She seemed to move with an anxious purpose. She didn't hesitate or glance in either of our directions.

I was recalling a type of "Morlock" character when she voiced a subtle...how could I describe...repeated hoots. As soon as she heard a dull, thudding sound, like a wooden branch tapped against a rail, she turned at the junction and disappeared into the gloom of the second tunnel.

Singer came over to my sight and signed, "She rang the doorbell. She's not alone."

It was in both our minds...to continue further could be dangerous.

Then again, to stay here and turn back was just not in our nature. One by one, we went further into the unknown. After several yards and changes in direction, from a cleft somewhere high on the mountains slope, daylight filtered through thick tree branches.

We were stunned to step into an arena-sized space and see full growth trees suddenly within a sort of plaza. One side of the cliff's face sloped away from its narrow upper opening down to its sixty-foot deep base flooring. Primitive dwellings, maybe past miner's quarters, were built with their back up against the wall and encircled by the narrow rails. Ladders had once allowed access, up into three separate mine openings. None of them would be visible from above. The surrounding, overhead rim looked treacherously like a sharp and precipitous gash.

Remaining concealed as much as possible, we waited. Soon enough we saw this female creature exit and enter one old dwelling with a bucket. It was not only for water. She removed bloodstained bandages and rinsed them out. Before long, she returned with two additional bundles…hand in hand, Singer whispered, "Children!"

This time, she turned and looked right in our direction.

I pulled his sleeve and motioned to return into the mine tunnel. "Singer, this is all kinda' crazy, but I could swear I heard her call for, "Help, Annie, help!"

"Me too, but it was inside my mind, not through the ears of my head."

"We're going back, tell Annie and find out what's going on."

* * *

Maggie, Sean, Jan, Singer and I listened together in the sewing room as Joseph, Betty and little Annie tended to farm animal chores.

Annie explained another of her long held secrets. "That's Esau's wife, Rachael, and her two little ones."

'Wife, Esau?" we all asked in unison.

"Sure! Did you see Esau?"

"No." I answered.

Singer added, "Only the mother and two children."

Annie asked for clarification, "And you said...blood-stained rags?"

"If you didn't see Esau, it means he's been hurt, maybe injured badly. I'll have to go see...alone!"

I answered, "That's right, you said a couple times to me and Maggie, 'Children, tsk, tsk, tsk! 'never think to ask the old folks for answers to questions.'"

With a satisfied smile for an important lesson being finally taught, Annie explained while beginning to gather first-aid materials, "Esau descended from those species, which Tiex and the Chinese families discovered. In 1859, after a solar flare whacked the earth and melted most of the telegraph wire into wildfires, a circus train had de-railed from warped rails. It crashed down in Oregon. Some of the animals survived, but a few escaped. The sideshow folks were left to their own survival; some of them teamed up. Esau's great-grandfather was a Russian giant and the Bearded Lady was his great-grandmother."

As we followed close behind her, she continued, "Considered only as 'freaks,' they secluded themselves from society, which was considerably more dangerous than living out among wilderness animals. Tiex and Lorena protected them as well as several Chinese friends."

Maggie asked, "Bear-man, Dremos, Russian Giants and circus Bearded Ladies, with whom else did they mate?"

"You forgot, Dragons. Maggie, please fetch a bottle of my brandy" then answered, "Mate? No, they were married. After the California Gold Rush Days, there was the story of Mercer Women, who came by wagons across the continent as mail-order brides from New York, for lonely loggers. One or two of the women were rather delicately described as, 'Great Ladies.'"

As Maggie packed away enough medical supplies, Annie smiled at a distant memory, "We, Sam, Tex, Daddy Red's mamma and I, spent most of one all-night, barbering, dressing and escorting Esau and Rachael down these stairs to be married the next morning. By sundown, both of them looked like they'd recovered a week old beard. Their hair grows fast and mostly all over, like bears or apes; but they're good folks just the same."

I shared amazement with everyone and asked, "Those tunnels are mine shafts, with rails and cars. What did they mine?"

"Those mineshafts are where they dug out emeralds."

"Dragon's eyes?"

"Rose was right when she said, 'You may be the sharpest blade in a bucket of knives.'"

"Singer and I felt a telepathic plea for your help."

"Rachael and Esau have a special, gift of language. I'm sure she knew you were both nearby, she didn't know if you were dangerous, so I'll explain who you all are."

Singer requested, "Shouldn't we go with you?"

"Perhaps later. Maybe…and I do mean, Maybe! You might be allowed to meet and help them."

"Maggie, Jan, it's time you come with me. If we need all you strong men, we'll let you know after we return."

Jan apologized and offered a Plan "B." "I'll drive down to Leavenworth with the children…you know, junk food and maybe rent some movies."

As Annie and Maggie drove up beyond the millpond and turned out of sight, Joseph and his sisters returned in time to ask a string of youngster's curiosity.

Their mamma simply said, "Get your coats," as she picked up her coat, keys and purse, "…and don't forget to go to the bathroom."

Sean smiled as they left. "I believe I'll keep Annie's rocking chair warm."

Singer's eyes twinkled, "Butts, didn't you say there's another tunnel system to explore?"

"We may need some climbing rope and gear."

In less than ten minutes, we were at the ruins' fireplace entry. First, I showed Singer the keypad for the trap door release. He marveled at the roar from the dragon's throat and we re-closed its panels. Entering Annie's stairway down to the old still and storage rooms, I re-closed the passageway after turning on the downstairs' light. It flashed once and burned out.

Pulling down our night goggle eyepieces, weapons at ready, we snapped a couple IRLs. These light wands only produced illumination of infrared wavelength. We started surveying beyond the wine rooms.

"Mr. Morgan, I've been called a drunk Indian more than once…I hope nothing happens to bring me down here alone."

"I hope you'll invite me as a chaperone if you do. Annie said, she didn't know about the rest of this cavern's system."

Looking around awhile, Singer added, "Tiex's Oriental friends kept busy as seven dwarfs."

"Butts, what are we looking for?"

While I sketched a crude schematic, I shrugged my shoulders, "I don't know exactly; Tiex and these folks who worked with him love puzzle boxes."

"OK…secret passage way, door, stairs, booby-traps, or hidden room, that leaves several options." Singer looked up, "…or maybe an attic?"

"Or, maybe a basement. I agree, but we shouldn't forget about something obvious and I can't see anything obvious in this chamber other than wine racks, the Still, those chairs at the end of that sixty-foot long table…"

"Huh…besides an old deck of poker cards and some chips, too, what is this long bundle upon the full table's length?"

Feeling the cloth, I exclaimed, "Silk?"

Singer carefully unfolded some of the middle section and began to uncover an embroidered image, "It's a great Oriental Dragon."

Nearly halfway down its length, the carefully folded silk fabric was reinforced with strong cords. These parachute sized cords continued to the end of the table where a large, woven, dust-shrouded basket perched.

I exclaimed with surprise, "It's a hot air balloon!"

"Where's the ventilation? The still had fire...the balloon, too, although it could be charged on the open ground level."

"I guess it's the shaft below the trap door." Striking a match, a draft made the flame whimper in the shaft's direction.

"What did you find during your first trip down here with the girls?"

"I climbed down the iron ladder while Maggie stayed above. It ended at the ledge beyond this gateway. Then, Annie came down the stairs with Maggie and turned on the light. I was a fair case of being startled."

"What were you about to do from the outside?"

"It was dark and I felt along the surface of both left and right hand walls to where I stood; I felt some sort of paneling on one side."

We opened the wrought iron doorway to the waterfall shaft. Today, the flow was not as full-force as from previous heavy snow melt. The sound of this immense stone throat was still loud and hollow, yet frightening.

Our eyepiece view was greenish-yellow from the IR-chem lights, but we had an eerie illumination on the alcove of the entry. On one side, carved bronze casting plates of a dramatic dragon's frozen ferocity, stared back at us out of brilliant emerald eyes.

I wondered out loud, "If this panel opens, it may be a narrow entry into another chamber."

"But, Butts...what or where is the key?"

Reaching up with my chem-light-stick to get the best view of the top edges and surrounding stonework, I grunted,

"I don't see a similar keypad like the fireplace locks. Other than this large ring hanging from the dragons' lower jaw, like a doors' knocker, no other part seems to be moveable."

Singer answered, "However, the entire panel could serve as a submarine sized passage, especially for smaller Oriental people."

I grasped the frames' edge and it suddenly released. It was a foot long part of the dragon's tail, which I'd pulled down like a lever. The water flow stopped, or was diverted somewhere else.

Grasping hard to the opposite walls of the alcove, Singer cautioned, "After your first trap-door experience, I'm a bit suspicious of where we're standing, or what we may have latched onto."

Handing one end of a rope to clip around his belt, Singer snapped the other end onto the bars of the door. "I'm going down the chute a bit."

The dragon's throat wasn't more than the balloon basket's diameter. Singer snapped a couple more IR-chemlights and placed them in his BDU's vest pockets. Carefully, he braced against the slippery, mossy sides, with one light stick clenched between his teeth, Singer rappelled off the ledge like a tunnel rat. About twelve feet down, out of sight because of the way the shaft bent and turned like a swimming pool's water-slide, he descended into the opening. He stopped and removed the IR-light, "Got another doorway down below."

"Hold on. I'll be right down." I secured another section of the rope to the doorknocker and followed down the winding, narrow course of this undulating throat. As soon as we stood beside each other, our lights illuminated a similar Dragons' face cast into a bronze-green patina of a larger door.

I sketched more diagrammed additions on my note pad. "This chamber's underneath, but to one side of the upper room where the Still is located...and here's the key."

Smearing off decades of mosses, I arranged the sliding segments and pushed the entire matrix plate into its doorframe. A now familiar click of a breech-loader sounded again.

Warily, we held onto our lifelines. The vault sized door slowly opened against years of complaining age. Stale air exhaled, like a blacksmith's bellows. New air rushed in from behind and above us, like a deep breath after waking up. This chamber's dome had the appearance of being the inside of a great stone bubble.

Sandy gravel at our feet sparkled with a strange combination. It was a shoreline, which encircled a crystal clear pool of icy water. Singer scooped up a handful for me to examine under his regular flashlight and asked, "Tiger-eyes and emeralds?"

The cavern's pond was fed from under the base of the wall where our passage had allowed our entry. Its subterranean outflow was in the direction of cliffs at the edge of Annie's valley. We hiked about ten minutes down its entire passage with sufficient ambient light. Somewhere up ahead we began to hear water falling. We could go no further. We found ourselves looking outside, through the main channel's flow. It joined the river's brink from the cliff beyond Annie and Sean's home.

I marveled to Singer, "A man on a large horse could enter or exit this chambered system of caves."

"Only if he had bird-man wings or riding Mobil's red Pegasus."

"Ok, let's check up in the other direction."

Perhaps another fifteen minutes passed as we climbed up the long incline from the entry. What we missed seeing above us was primarily due to the single lens night vision goggle's lack of depth perception. We had both paid more heed to our footsteps than our auditorium's ceiling. We could now discern several smaller grottos. Within each were suspended a dozen or more inert gargoyle-like shapes. They were all hung in a position similar to gigantic bats. "What the hell?"

CHAPTER TWELVE

Ascending the slope to the mine entrance, she heard, "Whew, Maggie, this is more of a stroll than I'm used to."

Concern filled her eyes as Aunt Annie said those words. Her color was a bit too pale and waxen. "Give me your satchel, and rest here a minute."

"I think I'll do just that...whew...for just a minute." Then giggling, said, "I guess my honeymoon night was a bit too strenuous."

Pulling out her plastic bottle of water, I handed it to her. She reached up to grasp the neck and it slipped right out of her fingers. "Tarnation, I'm sorry...land sakes!" She grasped it with her left hand and took a healthy drink. "I had a dream last night."

She had Maggie's concern before, but now she had all her attention for what her dream would reveal.

"I could fly like in kids' dreams. I swam with the wind and landed on the porch in front of Sean. He was sound asleep in my rocker...nice and peaceful. As I touched his shoulder, all of a sudden he looked young as when we'd first met. I heard someone behind me call my name and turned around to see several folks on the stairs and porch. Next thing I know, Sam steps forward and he shook Sean's hand like meeting old friends."

Her narrative left a cold hand on Maggie's heart as she went on, "Honey, Bristol is going to try and take you away from Buddy. I don't think he'll succeed because I saw Singer come up behind him in the dream."

Standing up and feeling much better, she said no more about the dream, "Come on, we need to tend to Esau."

The mineshaft's tunnels and railcar tracks opened into the hidden plaza. Daylight filtered through the thick canopy of full growth Fir trees. Beneath them, in their shadows were smaller trees sheltering new seedlings. Annie pressed her fingertips to her lips and whistled a birdcall of magpies.

Rachael appeared and returned a call of eagles.

At first sight of Rachael, Maggie felt apprehension and anxiety turn into relief for their arrival. Her children remained shy and mostly out of sight, yet full of curiosity at her presence with Annie.

Esau was lying on a bed in their back room. A gaping wound stretched from his shoulder to his belly. Four deep gashes looked just like a bear had inflicted them during an attack. His other shoulder and neck had deep bite marks. Annie immediately went to work on cleaning and applying antibacterial ointments. The brassy smell of blood was lightly mixed with their musky body odor. It wasn't a rank smell of untended personal hygiene; the smell had an ingredient of heavy sweat rubbed with cedar and evergreens.

Rachael's table was heaped with several varieties of new spring meadow greens and last years' parsnips, maybe even small varieties of potatoes. Her children finished eating and went into the side room to play.

Maggie heard an unmistakable tune of a Microsoft computer being turned on. Rachael sensed her questions and signed answers, which Annie translated. "Its power source is a prismatic grid of crystal sunbeams on our high-tech solar panel from fiber-optic sensors on the mountain's surface."

Annie began to carefully stitch up Esau's wounds...one by one. He never winced or complained. Maggie was more amazed at the deep bass sound of his words, "Thank you, Annie. That bear was fixing to attack my kids until I got in the way. She fled after Rachael arrived."

Looking intensely at me, he asked, "Who is this beautiful, young helper?"

"Esau, meet Maggie. Maggie, this is Esau."

They shook hands tenderly and Rachael greeted her with a huge hand placed on her breast, over her heart. She asked, "What are your children's names?"

Esau proudly answered, "Wookie and Weena, they're six and four years age."

From their side room, she heard more unmistakable sound effects of a Star Wars DVD. Looking back to Esau and Rachael, her look of amazement could only answer, "Yeah, why not?"

Annie informed her, "Your new friends are both endowed with several Ph.D.s in various fields of education. Besides holding a number of patents in Physics and Computer Science, they're learned in religion, politics and sociology."

Rachael signed a question, "Have you decided on who to vote for on this election?"

Maggie answered with a non-committal shrug, "It's the most difficult yet significant campaign in my voting lifetime."

Quickly signing another question, Rachael asked, "Who were the two soldiers following me home through the mine tunnel?"

She responded verbally, "My new husband, Buddy Morgan and his best friend, Singer. They would be honored to meet you."

"Is Buddy the one who broke up Bristol's features?"

"Yes."

Returning her smile, along with Rachael's sigh of humor, Esau answered, "Then, it will be my pleasure."

Annie added, "He and Singer are the only living descendants of Tiex and Lorena, besides me. Buddy found us after meeting Rose before she died in Benton, Arkansas. He met Singer on his drive here through Nevada."

"I remember the man named, Singer from a previous visit to Annie's before going into the Army."

Maggie answered, "They served as Snipers with Army Rangers in the countries of Uzbekistan, Afghanistan and Bagdhad."

"We need to meet if they wish to know the rest of Tiex's secrets."

With that said, Annie helped Rachael clean up Esau's soiled bandages and left instructions for further treatment. Rachael felt Esau's similar concern for Annie's age and health issues saying, "Let Maggie and Buddy come back next time with Singer. This trek can't be easy work for you. We can't tell you enough appreciation for all your love and care over all these years."

"Goodbye then." Annie hugged each and shared a longer stroke of hands on hearts.

Wookie and Weena gave Maggie a more modern hug and handshake then returned to their feature episode. At the door, Annie added, "A new sequel to 'National Treasure' is coming out next week. Do you want to check one out?"

"Thank you. Yes, but a bad storm is coming and we'll all be snowed in before the week is out."

Esau was right. By the time Annie and Maggie returned through the cavern's entry, snow flurries were falling as quickly as the temperature allowed. "Maggie, where are you and Buddy planning to go for your honeymoon?"

"Well, after a visit through Benton, Arkansas to visit Aunt Rose's grave, we'll stay in Denton, Texas until we can return home."

"Honey, home isn't going to be here for the rest of your life unless, you get to see other parts of the world first. Now Sean and I discussed the matter and we put a considerable trust fund in your name. Sean's arranged for much of this property to become a Scout Camp. There'll be enough left over even if you choose to go around the world."

Speechless and blushing, Maggie started to protest but Annie butted in with a, "Shush! Rose never called out for help from no one. It didn't sit fallow like a pile of boveen biscuits. It's all signed for you. Sean, bless his Leprechaun heart, is leaving Buddy a Pot-of-Gold."

Buddy and Singer were approaching the house as they arrived at Annie's porch. She added with secreted finality. "You and Buddy have a mission to perform. Tiex never was able to return the Dragon's Eyes. It has to be done. When you read the rest of Lorena's book, you and Buddy will understand. Esau needs to mend but Buddy and Singer have to learn what Esau will teach them about the 'Dragons Eyes'!"

Maggie's mind was in a whirl with Annie's information as she helped her up the stairs. Almost to the top, Annie stopped to catch her breath. She looked real pale. Concern filled Maggie's heart. She let go on her arm and paused to hug and kiss Buddy as Annie made it to the top stair alone. She stepped toward Sean. He was asleep in the same rocker as when we'd left. Annie began to cry, clutched at her throat and sat down on his lap to reach around Sean's shoulders and kiss him. She whispered, "Goodbye," and kissed him again before wrapping her arms around her knees and folding over in a release of emotions that ended with silence.

From the bottom of the stairs, they looked on with perplexed silence before realizing both had expired. If there were two holes in the night sky where their stars had once shone, the storm's cover kept them hidden behind the heavy snowfall.

* * *

We buried them, side by side, in the meadow near their home.

Singer's wife and children returned to their home. The next two weeks passed by under somber layers of storms, blizzards and mystically thick fog. Everything at the Valley of the Dragons was eroding. New fence lines, roads and garden furrows were rapidly flowing down stream until flushing off the cliffs into murky-brown, or milky-white waterfalls.

Bristol was not idle; while Esau met and instructed Buddy and Singer, Bristol's contacts in the government defense and black-ops departments went from ridiculous and incredulous into a frenzied tizzy-fit.

ALIAS TEX BUDA

At the end of two weeks, Singer returned to his family. Before he arrived, Jan disappeared. Kidnapped! Her ransom note read, "The Dragon's Eyes or your wife."

CHAPTER THIRTEEN

Bristol turned around to button up the fly of his denims after sprinkling the golden yellow blossoms of a low growing, but thorny cactus.

"Howdy! Bristol. My name's Crow Singer. My neighbors call me the Jack Mormon. No! Not Holy Joe and the Angel Macaroni, but they're good friends of mine."

Bristol clenched his fists till his knuckle's tendons snapped across the back of both hands.

Crow continued speaking soft, like not wanting to wake up any rattlers, "My last name's spelled with double O's, like both barrels of this ten gauge Buckshooter standing on top of that pretty looking frying pan you call a belt buckle, and Look! ...all spelled with those pearly gate letters, "Rodeo Champion."

Bristol's eyes measured the breadth of distance over to his piled up saddle, hat, holstered gun, carbine and Pecos tanned, hand made knee high boots.

"The only reason I'm reading you from the book, is over at the back room of Doc's home. You see, she's all covered up under a pure white linen veil. But, you and I have nothing else to talk about."

Sweat hardly makes a sound of its own to be heard or measured as a snarl of frustration escaped between the tobacco juice stains around Bristol's bearded mouth and mustache. A breath of the beginning of a string of cussing was silenced instantly in one shattered syllable.

Crow's pistol gripped Greenlee double barrel had only flicked upward for an instant, but bits of Bristol's broken teeth dribbled and fell as chips into the sand around the darned patches, where his toes had once poked through his socks.

"There's no confessing, or alibis expected. There's no last rites or wrongs to be administered, blessed, or passed. There's no last meal to be cooked, or any last words to be spoken, whispered, stuttered, stammered, or even prayed. So long!"

"Boom," was the only sound like a single echo against the back walls of the arroyo.

There was that one other sound. It was like when a store clerk threw two rolls of Washington quarters against the back wall to spill all over the tiled floor. Like as if they'd both broke open to jingle, spin and roll away after the first jangle of ricochets.

Folded over like a jack-knife, the dead man might have fit in any of most small cases for Hercules dynamite. Fact is, didn't need any of 'em to drop him into a crack in the cave floor.

The only mourners at Bristol's burial were a bunch of rattlers and scorpions 'quickly scurried out of the way as the shadow of the body plunged twenty feet down towards their dusty abode. The final amen, was the sound of a two-bit coin spinning to a final stop.

Singer sent Buddy a text message: "Got him. It was Bristol."

CHAPTER FOURTEEN

Crow Singer gathered his children after their mother's funeral and began a world journey, through India, to Nepal.

In Denton, Texas, Maggie and I shared several early morning coffee calls at Amy and Joey's Jupiter House. Denton's Arts and Jazz Festival garnered over 200,000 visitors during its three-day weekend. Saturday couldn't have been more perfect.

Maggie phoned Daddy Red and her brothers often. Growing up in one community or state, does not make distant travelers immune to homesickness.

Joey and Amy's coffee shop was packed throughout campus final's week. Amy asked Maggie and I one morning, "We're taking a two-week vacation break. Joey and I talked it over and wondered if you'd agree to house-sit our upstairs loft?"

Having bounced around as overnight guests with several friends for the previous two weeks, we were wearing thin of not being alone. We'd wake up when others needed to do so. More often than not, every breakfast was at Ruby's Diner, for a buffet, or simply coffee and cakes at the Jupiter House. We wished for the privacy of our own sort of suite. The Radisson Hotel was no longer open. Denton's motto could easily be four 'nuf's: "Near enough; far enough; large enough; small enough." With that said, Denton's one fine hotel was gone, the bus service could be better but often is, "maybe."

ALIAS TEX BUDA

Sunrise poured into Joey and Amy's loft on our second private morning. I let Maggie sleep in, left a note and slipped out to complete an errand. When I returned, she was awake reading more of the old book that Granny Annie had given her. She was laughing. "I couldn't stop laughing with reading another part. Listen to this."

"A small town bully met Tiex and Crow while terrorizing a meek local woman. By the next morning, the town marshal and a deputy found Mr. Bully, naked as a sleeping baby, huddled in a fetal ball, sucking his thumb. A sewing thread was whipped stitched through his nose, like a bull ring; the other end of thread had been knotted through the flesh of his thumb.

"The town marshal and deputy, through side-splitting laughter asked, "What in Hell's name happened?"

"During their knee-slapping guffaws, the bully explained all could be remembered. 'Some little bearded guy was stitching gloves…he wasn't lookin' where he was going…poked me in the back, he did. I grabbed him by the throat and let have at him with a backhand. I could feel 'im shaking but he stopped still. He stuttered some kind of curse and his blue eyes turned white as snowcaps. Next thing I felt was as if I was squeezing a melting icicle. I looked down at my feet and 'could see I'd pissed a puddle down my leg. Fast as I could tie piggin' string on a calf's three legs, something like fire touched my palm and nostrils…like a pinched nose ring…before I could blink twice, he was gone! But, just as sudden, he was there again… with my hand still clutched 'round 'is scrawny neck…He winked and whispered, 'Say, Bullshit!'

"'Bullshit,' said the deputy.

"Just like that, Mr. Bully smacks a solid fist into 'is own nose!

"Before the bone and cartilage had finished crunching, the Marshal repeated his deputy's disbelieving words, 'Bullshit!'

"Flattened nose and blooded fist repeated a second resounding, 'Smack!'

"'Can you tell us what he looked like?'

"Through a double-barrel bucket of frustrating tears, Mr. Bully cried out in blind rage, 'I don't know…I can't remember nuthin'!'

"By sundown, the local saloon was three rows deep…at least the far end of the bar, when a flat-nose-bandaged bully walked up and demanded a beer. Just as he lifted it off the surface of the dark stained wood, someone at the far end phrased a carefully expressed, 'Bullshit,' in the direction of the upturned mug.

"Yup! Beer, blood and glass resounded in another crunch. Echoes of the delightful word resounded off the saloon walls, amid cheers till near' everyone pissed in their own pants. The ridiculed, laughingstock of the community and any part of the country where the phrase, 'Bullshit', might be uttered within his sorry-ass earshot, was never seen again."

Maggie rocked with laughter, then suddenly dissolved into tears.

"What's the matter, honey?" I asked, alarmed.

"I'm homesick. I want to get up and fix your breakfast and wash our clothes and sit on our own porch in the peace and quiet of sunsets."

I tried to soothe her with, "We'll go somewhere else…be alone…Turner Falls maybe in Oklahoma or visit Grandma Rose's orchard…"

"I like it here…I don't like all the levels of campus conversations after dark…I mean…I don't mean, let's leave, I'd…I'd…I don't know."

Inspiration is a welcome friend. "Do you like to go fishing?"

"Well, yeah."

"Well, I remembered, you and Annie always caught more and bigger fish than any of Sean, Daddy Red or your brothers…"

"We didn't pack any fishing poles or gear, remember?"

"Yeah, right…but…"

"We don't have a fishing license."

"I'll make some up."

"That's forgery."

"I meant fishing gear and lures."

"You can do that?"

"Singer saw me catch some good fish in Nevada with no more than six feet of monofilament line and a made-up lure over a hook."

"I thought Singer didn't eat fish?"

"He doesn't. He ate the rabbits."

"What kind of a lure?"

"My friend, Grandpa Jack, showed me how to take a small piece of scrap, tooling, calfskin leather and slice it before plaiting a five-strand mystery braid ten times."

"The old grandpa with the scruffy beard?"

"Yeah, the storybook writer that stitched hats and gloves until arthritis got too bad. He calls his new leather lures, 'Jupiter Bugs…they're outta' this world.'"

Hugging her into a rocking chair's soothing ball of comforter and careful kisses, I whispered, "Anyway, after pinching on a couple two-pronged shiny metal spots, he folded it in half lengthwise. Something because of the braid formed a curved, sort of skirt, around his bass hook. The braiding resembles a tail on crawdads, shrimp or lobsters. When the leather's wet, it moves easily with a fluid motion like flapping."

Maggie's eyes began shining brighter. "We'll, if it's made of tooling leather, it will soak up moisture. We may have to rub it in something stinky?"

"We could ask Kroger's fish market for some lobster water to marinade the lures overnight?"

"You're good, that's why I love you more each day."

"Buddy, maybe it's easier than making our own. Let's visit Jack this morning and maybe he'll make you some."

"Does someone in the Mini-Mall sell fishing poles?"

"If they don't, McBrides Pawn Shop will have some. Today's Sunday, we'll check them tomorrow morning. Did you forget what today is?"

Handing her a pretty bouquet and card, she cried again. It said, "Happy Mother's Day." Wiping tears after a slow, glowing kiss, she slipped out of her nightgown and cuddled in my lap with the whisper, "Crying again she sniffled, "Aunt Annie was the only mom I knew. I've waited a long time to become a mother."

The old grandpa, the leather-braided-fishing-lure guy, was

seated outside the Jupiter House Coffee shop when Maggie and me were resting our saddle-sores a week after Mother's Day.

"Ya'll been fishing last weekend?"

With a smile and Maggie's blush, I answered, "We haven't gone out of the apartment most of since we saw you last."

"It's been hot and muggy, near a hundred degrees…I don't blame you and pretty as Maggie is, I'd say it's more important to bring up grandchildren, who have two legs and no tails."

We all laughed at good wit.

Maggie added, "Maybe this weekend. We haven't found any poles, yet."

An old sort of fellow anyway, he answered, "Shaw! I just got in a batch of Sparks Hot Rods. They're entire cane-pole fishing rigs. I'd be honored if you'll try this new design lure jacket. It's called, the 'May-Bee,' 'cause my ninety-four-year-old Dad thought it was the biggest 'maybe' I'd had in forty hard-luck years of leather-craft designing. I've designed hat and cap kits, glove kits, miniature monkey hats and braided leather rings…none of them has ever had the potential of these silly leather hook jackets."

Just about that time, a sorry quad of butt-high, pants-dressed teenagers arrived. Jack greeted the smallest kiddo, "Well, hell, Tinker-Bell, I see you ain't had to get them pretty blond curlylocks burr-cut, yet."

That insult kid must have had a sorry set of parents or even grandparents. They never got the lesson about civil public manners correctly applied to his education; he retorted with a sneer. "Quit calling me that!" He then hacked up a piss-ant mouthful and spit it on the sidewalk of where Amy and Joey's front door opened up.

Jack was set where a plastic bucket marked, "Dogua" had quenched someone's previously thirsty pets. Grandpa Jack had a left hand up to hold the door open and the little Spittite visibly blanched. Tinker-Bell lifted his right hand in case of need to defend himself. Grandpa Jack smiled as he took hold of the proffered hand-shake, even if it wasn't intended. In a blink of an eye, Tinker-Bell's hand was raised up and over his bleached-blond, spiked hair-do and it twirled the kiddo like a rock and roll ballerina. Next, Grandpa Jack twisted this youngster's arm up behind his back, let go of the door and clasped a pinch of boney thumb and finger on the sorry Kiddo's shoulder-neck muscle. It must have got the boy's attention. Jack's words of education proceeded to be pronounced as the rest of the gang deserted their group leader.

"Now, I've been told this here muscle was given to parents and pissed-off teachers. It doesn't bruise and it's a lot closer to your pea-brain than whacking on your butt…"

The captured prey struggled and Jack pinched harder. Tears and regret didn't cleanse the kid's stream of perverted profanities.

Maggie even blushed and I wasn't pleased, but Grandpa Jack simply let go of his hand-shake grip and grasped the low-slung waistband of crotch-high fashion jeans and gave the belial lad a swift jerk up off the ground. Tinker-Bell struggled with flailing hands and wildly kicking feet as patrons and passer-byes began to gather around the activity. Over the bucket of dog-water, Jack lifted its handle and asked me to fetch it to his hand.

"Yes, sir!" I answered while smiling just as two bicycle cops rode up on their sets of police mobility. I swear, they simply didn't hinder the application of this lesson of civil behavior. As we all watched, Jack poured the water onto Tinker-Bell's exposed butt and bare, florescent-white legs since his britches had slid just past his knees.

Pronouncing one last benediction, Grandpa Jack patiently prayed, "Now, son..." Tinker-Bell writhed even more... "If'n I had a corncob, I'd probably shove it up your lily-whites and take a picture to post on that new-fangled view-tube for a warning to all your likes of friends. We will no longer tolerate: foul public speech or expectorations ...since the good Lord didn't provide a nearby corn-cob, you'll be spared that embarrassment...but lily-butts, if you don't change your ways and realize I'm your best friend..."

Reclamping his neck, Tink was still crying and screaming such foul profanities as to make hardened war veterans shrink.

"Well, I can't save you from the cost of your words..." Letting loose of his shoulder muscle pinch, he clamped a boney finger and thumb onto Tink's nose. The foul words stopped spewing forth like a bad diarrhea. Tink had to breathe through his mouth. "Learn wisdom in your youth or learn it the hard way behind barred doors you're heading one-way towards. All we're trying to teach you is how proud we are ...see all these American folks gathered...proud we are that you'll take this lesson to heart and act with civil and decent manners while in the presence of folks who bled or saw their friends die to give you freedom and rights."

The policemen finally said, "That's enough. We'll take it from here and call his parents from the station. Don't be surprised if they'll try to sue or charge you with assault on a minor...but, confidentially, I can't think of any local judges who wouldn't throw such a case out their window and shake your hand as they walk you out the doors of court."

Grandpa Jack was shaking some after the dose of adrenalin. He invited, "Y'all come with me. I want you and Maggie to have a look-see at eight antique rifles."

Look-see we did and my amazement was not alone. These old rifles had come from over a century old, lost trove, of cached weapons. The British East India Company had turned the four-story Royal Palace in Khatmandhu, Nepal into an Armory. A history lesson in Nineteenth Century weapons had been preserved by thick dust from local brick factories and Himalayan foothills climate.

Maggie recognized one of the same like as Grannie Annie's, "Brown Bess."

Grandpa Jack had received a book printed about the story of the find. Several principal figures and political leaders were recognizable. However one name struck us more with awe and silence. Of four regiments, which tried to fight their way into the great valley of the Khatmandhu and Bramaputra River, only one succeeded. Of the other three regiments destroyed by Ghurka warriors, only one life was spared. It was a commander, so disgraced by the losses, that the shame hounded him into obscurity. His last name was Ochterlony—the same as Bristol's middle name. The dishonor had ended there.

THE END

ALIAS TEX BUDA

TATTERS

((All the tatters saved from accidental discharge of Grannie Annie's Mr. Ten-gauge Greenlee))

(Lorena Annapurna's notes during sea voyage with Mormons, which does not include Romance story of Tiex Buda and Lorena Annapurna…from 20th Sep. 2007—5th Oct 2007.)

More drowned than half-alive, Grandpa washed up on the Nor'eastern shore of Scotland. Grandmothers' parents found this mercenary as they collected salvage from an unfortunate capsized shipwreck. Sheltering him at their Inn, the two isolated youngsters fell in love. Having shortly recovered, he returned to the mainland of Denmark, unaware that three seasons later, a strapping baby boy was born on the side of a road, during a late October storm.

She only knew her lover's first name, Johann. Little other about the infant's father was known, except for the maps he carried from a shop in Hamburg of "Matth-Hesse and Sonne." Thus grandpa's name became Ian, or Sean Matheson, rather than Johann.

Papa, Hugh Matheson, Sean's youngest son, was born along the highlander shores of the Northwestern British Isles. His family raised the small kine of the clans, as well as tending sheep for wool and goats for skins to be tawed into fine material for making gloves and garments.

To say that was all anyone of us did was a fool's determination. We hunted deer with the hounds my father raised. Scottish hemp was grown for rope, sail cloth and evening bowls of sweet savory smoke after dinners.

One year, while putting green applets from under June-drop-trees, the idea was hatched to take their entire herd of Scottish cattle to markets in the south of England. A major problem to this drive of shaggy beasts, was how to get through the southern clans property without paying tolls.

Knowing these clans held fierce rivalries towards one another, messengers were sent with rumors of trespassing raids to either clans' opposite borders. While defenders hurried to those far regions, our herds were gathered and pushed south through the now unprotected middle lands.

The prices paid for these cattle were indeed higher. With silver money in his poke and a young spirit ready for adventure with nothing to fear, Hugh met Dinah, my mother, in Glastonbury, England.

He loved to sing and upon hearing her melodious tunes floating down from an upstairs window while she brushed her gorgeous hair, he joined in with his rich baritone voice.

Familiar with her song's lyrics, like a serenade, he received a promise for a visit after a proper introduction.

Young Hugh courted her seriously for a winter season and proposed. Her papa's shop in town sold tanned leathers and goods. His initial disapproval changed after observing this young man's entrepreneurial fabrication of hats and gloves.

Besides making his own patterns, Papa's Highlander inventive mind allowed him to design a peculiar device to clamp pieces of glove pattern fingers together. Along the top edges of his clamps, V-shaped serrated teeth provided even spacing for precisely intricate stitching.

Their problems were only beginning. Royal sealers visited the shop and threw all their finished gloves and goods in the street before lighting them afire.

Mama was a vivacious, red-haired glove-making seamstress. Her name was Dinah. She followed in the footsteps of a tradition honoring her mothers and grandmothers.

For centuries back to Jesus' grandmother and her daughter, Mary, family stories were repeatedly told while sitting in stitching circles outside the cottages in the hamlets where she'd been born and grew up.

"…In a ship, without sails and oars, a Cyrenian had rescued the doomed passengers after the High Priest's brother had Jesus' brother James killed.

…Jesus' mother, Mary and uncle Joseph of Arimathea, wives, Martha and her sister Mary, were cared for and safely transported with a few others to separate destinations of Gaul and the Isles of the Sea, from the port now known as Marseilles, where Martha stayed.

Joseph of Arithemea, provided them a home in Avalon, which his famed nephew had built without human hands. This shelter for his sister's only daughter, Mary, and Mary Magdelene lived out their days in Britannia's lush, green climate.

Hugh's family tales included lineage tracing back through Zedekiah's daughters, Jeremiah, and centuries earlier, one of Judah's twin sons named, Harris, although the backwards spelling was pronounced, Zarah.

After Dinah's father had the tragic encounter with the Royal Sealers, his family joined Hugh for the trek north. After their arrival, they began working with the glove-making guilds of Aberdeen, Dundee and Embro, Scotland.

Mormon missionaries taught strange tales of a translated, ancient gold book. They joined their church and packed up patterns, shears, and families, then on June 1, 1862, boarded the ship *John J. Boyd*, bound for America.

Earlier families had also migrated to the new world. Papa's great-uncle was partner in a map-making shop across from Edinburough, Scotland, in Hamburg, Germany. From up at Dundee, our cousin's families raised the hemp, from which to make rope for ship-builders. These joint family businesses prospered until the Scottish rebellion of 1745.

Visiting relatives oft brought clan-gatherings around the great wall fireplace. We heard some state politics, but gladly, more tales of mapmaker's adventures on the high seas.

Legends were told and retold of wars and warriors, loves found, loves and lives lost, and treasures buried. We sweetened our dreams with steaming plum puddings dripping with sour sauce, or hot apple pie slices that were a full four fingers thick.

Hugh's distant uncle, Johann Mattheson, was a friend and musician of renown to compatriots, such as George Fredrich Handel, Telemann and Johann Sebastian Bach Jr.

Johann Mattheson took a music teacher position with the British Emmisary, Cyril Wich. Later, Johann secured the position of choirmaster for the Hamburg Dom-Kirche, Johann began printing blank sheet music pages on that uncles larger map-making press.

Johann Mattheson, while being loyal to his mentor Cyril Wich, boarded a ship bound from Hamburg's harbor for Scotland, and discovered it was laden with arms and munitions destined for the Scottish rebels. Suddenly our family name became synonymous with Judas and Traitor.

In Hamburg, Johann Mattheson, with the help of his British wife, had begun printing new-fangled translations of political letters into something he called, newspapers. *The Bee, The Tatler,* and *Der Spiegel,* had begun a series of advertisements asking for trade guilds and craftsmen to bring their families and tools to the new world lands. Hugh, Dinah, their parents and young families took flight for their lives in the wake of wars and turbulence.

They packed up their patterns and long-shears and began the trans-oceanic voyage across the dangerous North Sea. Previous storms had claimed many loads of merchants' cargo, which was destined to distant markets along riverside centers of commerce.

Not finding a solution to their supply problem, the notion of classified ads in continental newspapers, of bringing the trades and crafts to land grants, was pure inspiration. With many other trades families, survival took on a whole different perspective.

Painfully immediate as a toothache, seasickness or severe illness claimed both lives of infants or aged. Seafarer prayers are about as close to God as mothers in childbirth. Both are born through torrents of salt-water and blood …both are uplifted by Spirit and daylight…both are filled with the price of Joy as rainbows after deluge.

* * *

Around the time Judah, secured a wife named Tamar for his eldest son, Judah's baby-sister Dinah had been bereft of her newly promised to be married husband.

Dinah and Judah's elder brothers, Simeon and Levi, had treacherously slain the men of a village named, Shecam.

What happened to Dinah? Was she pregnant? After Simeon and Levi removed Dinah from the household of Hamor, Shecam's ruler, where did she go? Where did she have her child? Was it the daughter found by a prophet, all covered in newborn blood and ants? Was she the baby Jeremiah recorded was raised into the most beautiful young woman of the then known world? She isn't mentioned in the names of those who later go to Egypt, where Joseph was ruler.

Judah's two oldest sons died. He promised his daughter-in-law, Tamar, some such when his youngest son was old enough, she would be married to him so that he could begat children for his deceased elder brother. Judah seemed to have forgotten. Tamar took matters into her own actions. She became pregnant with twin sons unbeknownst to Judah, who had unwittingly fathered them. Their names, Zarah and Perez are mentioned in the names of Jacob's family, who go down to Egypt, where Joseph is Pharaoh's principal chief governor.

* * *

Bone weary, bandaged, beaten, the mercenary from Buda, near Peste, in what is now the country of Hungary, had fought viciously with other Ghurka warlords to protect the King and Prophet of Nepal against Chinese invaders. The years beginning European 1800's found places for many mercenaries to war for riches. In this young Everest's case, he fought hard to live and survive long enough to hold his princess bride's newborn child. His fathers and grandfathers were whittled from Hessian woods and Highland stones. Even Everest's great-grandfathers had served the Kings of Sweden, being born of Viking lineage, before settling in Buda, near Peste, the homeland of his forefathers.

The Son of Buda brought knowledge from his lineage of arms and artificers of weapons used for war. The ancient sword and stone casting would not work for the new irons and Sky metals. Steel and grains of the casting stones would seal fast together. The swords called Khukris, descendants of Iberia and Alexander The Great's, "Falcatta," could not be removed from the stones from within which they were cast.

From wars in China, he and his beleaguered comrades had made their way across the rim of heaven, then down the valley between the Mothers, Annapurna, and Shagarmatha, Queen of all mountains upon the face of the Earth below which they we're standing. With them, their spoils of war included: tempered swords made from many welded layers and folding to make razor-sharp steel edges.

Shelter and protection were finally theirs to savor, sleep and give silent praise of thanks to their several Gods, or God. Within the valley of the Yeti and the Cave of Dragons, all veritably collapsed wherever they sat. Using whichever stone or slanted surface, they died into slumber until the next midday sliver of sunlight raced as a flying lance between the clefts of morning and cliffs of dusk.

The Cave of Dragons was a sacred place of endowment for every young Ghurka lad to pass into manhood. Never had women's feet touched the shores of the Kali River rapids. Home of Snow Lions and Dremos, because of the stillness, isolation and deepest shadows, its hidden entrance began behind a waterfall whose power could break weak backs, shoulders and arms. Caverns above this great waterfall deepened along separate passageways of gravel and sand. Its stone slabs were prized to split, engrave, and molten their famed bronze swords.

Each proven warrior had previously been privileged to carry away large enough slabs for casting, and only one other small fist sized hone to sharpen their swords with their entire life-long.

"To live by the sword and sleep by it, too, did not mean, to die by it, except in the last breath of life, in the arms of their families and wives.

The last gifts from the Sacred Lair were the eyes of Dragons from generations past. Given to worthy men, whichever kinds of gems blessed them with each or every several endowments of: Wisdom, Discernment, Strength of Dremo, and Stealth of the Snow Lion, sure-footed swiftness of the mountain goat, charity and fortune, faith and healing,

ALIAS TEX BUDA

protection, and invisibility and knowledge.

Some successful, young initiates may find one dragon's eye, some others only five, yet others, ten dragon's eyes and be blessed with their several keys of power, or gifts of Spirit.

Never had the Mother of the mountain granted one man all twelve eyes of the six-headed dragon, until Everest, the Son of Buda.

The fairest daughter of the King of Nepal's Royal family was given him to marry. Although he could have married more wives, as their culture practiced, he was devoted only to this one woman.

His faith was anciently Christian, although his black-sheep fore-fathers were outcast from The Knights of Templar to the fringes of Eastern civilization's small industrial town of, Buda, near Peste.

* * *

(Lorena Annapurna Notes 28 May 2007)
Alias Tex Buddah 1809-1909

Son to a Black Watch Highlander father – lived in Khatmandu, Nepal…born three or four years prior to Nepal's invasion of and war with India from 1813 to 1816…his mother's Buddhist heritage nurtured him in the absence of his father's presence during mercenary conflicts and military campaigns…

ABOUT THE AUTHOR

Along the path of his life, JIM MATHESON has been a soldier, a singer, a teacher, a disciple, a maker of hats and gloves, a spinner of stories and a teller of tales. He is still most of these and many more. His first book, *Lil' Bit's Heart of Christmas*, was first published in 2003 and was reprinted several times before inclusion in an anthology published in 2008. *A Lil' Bit of Jim Matheson: Lil' Bit's Heart of Christmas and other Stories* contains all of Jim's published novellas and previously unpublished work. He is now the spokesman for Texbuda Brands, a line of men's sportswear, and the inventor of Smilin' J Brand handmade leather fishing lures. Life is interesting.

CPSIA information can be obtained
at www.ICGtesting.com
Printed in the USA
BVHW060150190720
583718BV00007B/121